WAYSIDE & WOODLAND

WILD FLOWERS

© AA Media Limited 2011
Written by James Hall

Produced for AA Publishing by D & N Publishing, Baydon, Wiltshire

Commissioning editor at AA Publishing: Paul Mitchell
Production at AA Publishing: Rachel Davis

Printed and bound in China by C&C Offset Printing Co. Ltd

A CIP catalogue record for this book is available from the British
Library.

ISBN 978 0 7495 6925 9
     978 0 7495 6932 7 (SS)

The contents of this publication are believed correct at the time of
printing. Nevertheless, the publishers cannot be held responsible
for any errors or omissions or for changes in the details given in this
guide or for the consequences of any reliance on the information
provided by the same. This does not affect your statutory rights.

Published by AA Publishing, a trading name of AA Media Limited,
whose registered office is Fanum House, Basing View, Basingstoke,
Hampshire RG21 4EA. Registered number 06112600.

A04089
theAA.com/shop

CONTENTS

INTRODUCTION

Many of Britain's wild flowers are adapted to life in woods or in glades and woodland edges. They include some of our most familiar and well-loved wild flowers, as well as some plants that are rare, unusual or even downright strange.

The catch-all phrase 'waysides' includes grassy verges and roadside banks, hedgerows and hedge bottoms. It may include areas of drably named (but often unexpectedly rich in wildlife) scrub. Some of our most attractive orchids, for example, actually prefer scrub – so don't ignore it. Wild flowers are often left completely to their own devices in odd forgotten corners. Such places, on the margins of our often overly tidy world, deserve to be explored and cherished.

The *AA Spotter Guide to Wayside & Woodland Wild Flowers* covers 182 species. These include the most widespread representatives likely to be found in suitable habitats in England, Wales and Scotland. In addition, some rare and tricky-to-find wild flowers are included.

A full page is devoted to each species. The text has been written in a concise manner so that as much information as possible can be packed into the space available. Each species entry begins with the common English name and is followed by the species' scientific name. For ease of use, the subsequent text has been divided into sections: **FACT FILE**, which covers the species' size, habitat preferences, flowering period and habit (its overall appearance and growing style); **IDENTIFICATION**, which describes its appearance and gives detailed information about flowers and leaves in particular; **STATUS AND COMMENTS**, which describes where the species occurs in the region, and provides an indication of its abundance or scarcity; and **KEY FACT**, which gives further information, or a brief description of a very similar plant to help differentiate them. A photograph of the plant accompanies the text.

HEDGEROW CRANE'S-BILL,
a colourful wayside plant.

BRITAIN'S WOODLANDS IN spring can rank among the most lovely natural sights in the world. Sheets of Bluebells and Primroses are still, thankfully, a common scene in many woods, and generations of us have gone down to the woods in April and May to soak up the colours and scents. But such sights and places are far fewer today than in our grandparents' time. Changing ideas about woodland management, and what tree species were most commercially viable, resulted in millions of hectares of native broadleaved trees being replaced with conifers in the first half of the 20th century. These dark, uniform tree factories shade out the wild flowers, often resulting in a woodland floor that is little better than a desert. Other woodlands, often with documented histories going back hundreds of years, were simply grubbed out to become arable farmland.

The good news is that today many surviving native broadleaved woodlands are cherished and cared for, and there is a movement to re-establish such areas where possible. For many years the Woodland Trust (www.woodlandtrust.org.uk) has been quietly buying up woods, and also planting tens of thousands of hectares with native trees. The National Trust (www.nationaltrust.org.uk) is embarking on long term plans to restore many of its woodlands to their previous flowery glory, and Wildlife Trusts around the country (www.wildlifetrusts.org) are engaged in ambitious projects to enhance existing woodlands and to join up scattered fragments into much larger wildlife-rich areas.

Because they are relatively undisturbed, roadside hedgerows and verges can be excellent places to look for a wide variety of wild flowers, but only if the verge is safe from traffic, and has not been sprayed with 'weed' killers or insensitively cut at the wrong time of year. Fortunately, many local councils and other authorities are now becoming more conscious of the wildlife value of such places.

Forgotten corners and wasteland can also be brilliant for wild flowers, but these uncelebrated places often suffer from our modern mania for tidying things up, resulting in manicured, sterile stretches of mown grass. So, encourage a more relaxed attitude to 'scrub', and generally untidy patches in your area, including in your own garden!

THESE DAYS IT is sometimes hard to be sure whether a plant is a native wild flower (one that grows naturally in our region) or has been introduced or spread by man. In truth, the distinction between any given species' native range and where its spread has been assisted is often blurred and impossible to discern.

Flowers themselves may be colourful, ornate and pleasing to the human eye, but their role is strictly functional. They comprise colourful petals and less colourful sepals, and, most importantly, the plant's sex organs. Their job is to maximise the chances of successful pollination (fertilisation). Although there are exceptions, most plants produce separate male and female structures in the same flower, although typically they go to great lengths to ensure that self-pollination does not occur. Pollen (containing male sex cells) is produced on structures called anthers, borne on long stalks called filaments; collectively these two structures are referred to as stamens. The female part of a flower comprises the stigma (which receives the pollen), which is connected to a basal ovary by a stalk-like style.

Although some plants rely on the wind to carry their pollen, the majority of our most familiar wild flowers use insects for this purpose. Attracted by the colourful petals and bribed by the reward of nectar, insects such as bumblebees, hoverflies, butterflies and moths unwittingly transfer pollen from one flower to the next one visited.

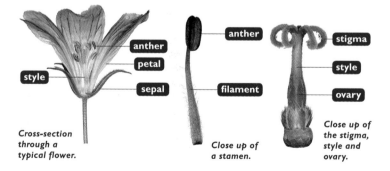

anther
petal
style
sepal

Cross-section
through a
typical flower.

anther
filament

Close up of
a stamen.

stigma
style
ovary

Close up of
the stigma,
style and
ovary.

Annual Plant that germinates, grows and sets seed within a single growing season.

Anther Pollen-bearing structure of a flower.

Axil Angle between the plant stem and the upper surface or stalk of a leaf.

Basal rosette Rosette of leaves at the base of a plant.

Berry Fleshy, soft-coated fruit containing several seeds.

Biennial Plant that takes two years to complete its life cycle.

Bract Modified, often scale-like leaf found at the base of flower stalks in some species. A small secondary bract is called a bracteole.

Calcareous (of soils) Containing calcium; usually from chalk or limestone.

Deciduous Plant whose leaves fall in autumn.

Disc florets Small flowers found at the centre of inflorescences of members of the daisy family.

Filament Stalk on which the anther is carried.

Floret Small flower.

Fruits Seeds of a plant and their associated structures.

Lanceolate Narrow and lance-shaped.

Leaflet Leaf-like segment or lobe of a leaf.

Lobe Projection on a leaf (larger than a tooth).

Nut Dry, often hard fruit containing a single seed.

Palmate (of leaves) With finger-like lobes arising from the same point in a hand shape.

Perennial Plant that lives for more than two years.

Pinnate (of leaves) With opposite pairs of leaflets on a central stem.

Petals Inner segments of a flower; often colourful.

Sepal Outer, usually less colourful structures surrounding the reproductive part of a flower.

Stamen Collective name for an anther and filament.

Stigma Female structure of a flower that receives pollen.

Style Stalk-like structure of a flower connecting the stigma and ovary.

Tooth Small projection on the margin of a leaf.

Trifoliate Leaf with three separate lobes.

Umbel Umbrella-like arrangement of flowers.

HOP
Humulus lupulus

SIZE Height to 6m **HABITAT** Hedgerows, rough ground, old gardens **FLOWERING PERIOD** Jul–Aug **HABIT** Climbing perennial

KEY FACT Hops are native to Britain, and have been used for centuries to flavour and enhance beer. The tender young shoots are delicious when lightly cooked and served with butter.

IDENTIFICATION
Leaves are deeply lobed, with three to five lobes; borne on tough, prickly, square stems; dark green. Stems grow clockwise up through shrubs and trees. Male and female flowers are produced on different plants: males are yellow, on clustered stems; females are tiny and hidden within cone-like scales that become the well-known hop fruit.

STATUS AND COMMENTS
Locally common, but needs tall, strong shrubs and trees up which to grow. It can be an escape from cultivation (especially in S counties, where it is grown commercially on a large scale), so may be found in seemingly unlikely places.

SPOTTER'S CHART

LOCATION	DATE/TIME

FACT FILE SIZE **Forms a ball up to 1.5m across** HABITAT **Trees such as apples, poplars and willows** FLOWERING PERIOD **Feb–Apr** HABIT **Semi-parasitic, tree-living evergreen**

IDENTIFICATION
Leaves are oval, blunt, leathery, up to 4cm long; shades of green. Flowers are tiny, green, in inconspicuous clusters. Fruits are semi-translucent whitish berries. No other plant looks or grows like Mistletoe.

KEY FACT This strange plant, held in reverence for thousands of years and still a major part of Christmas celebrations, sometimes grows in great abundance, such as in the cultivated apple orchards of the Somerset Levels.

STATUS AND COMMENTS
Mistletoe has a patchy distribution throughout England and Wales, being common in some areas and absent from others. Absent from Scotland.

SPOTTER'S CHART

LOCATION	DATE/TIME

IVY
Hedera helix

FACT FILE

SIZE Height up to 30m **HABITAT** Woods, hedges, scrub; on trees and on the ground **FLOWERING PERIOD** Sep–Dec **HABIT** Climbing, clinging, creeping evergreen

KEY FACT Ivy is a superb plant for wildlife, providing nectar for insects late in the year, berries for birds in the depth of winter and year-round shelter for a host of creatures.

IDENTIFICATION
Leaves are of two sorts: three- or five-lobed on non-flowering stems; arrow-shaped and wavy on flowering stems; both are dark glossy green. Flowers are tiny, greenish, in globe-shaped heads; scented. Fruits are black berries in globe-shaped clusters.

STATUS AND COMMENTS
Common throughout Britain. It can tolerate very deep shade, and will carpet a woodland floor as well as growing up the trees. It climbs by means of tiny, clinging, fibrous rootlets.

SPOTTER'S CHART

LOCATION	DATE/TIME

COMMON NETTLE
Urtica dioica

FACT FILE

SIZE Height to 1m HABITAT Waste ground,
verges, disturbed ground FLOWERING PERIOD Jun–Oct
HABIT Upright perennial

KEY FACT

Also called Stinging Nettle,
this is a very useful plant despite its stings. The
tender young leaves can be cooked and eaten,
and the plant has been used to make fabrics and
as an ingredient in medicines. It is also a foodplant
of some butterfly species.

IDENTIFICATION
Leaves are oval, toothed, with a pointed tip; they
are stalked, 6–8cm long and carried in opposite
pairs. Flowers are green, in pendulous catkins; male
and female flowers are produced on separate plants.
The whole plant is armed with stinging hairs,
which cause the sometimes very painful stings.

STATUS AND COMMENTS
Widespread and often extremely common throughout Britain, colonising
newly disturbed ground and often
growing in sizeable patches.

SPOTTER'S CHART

LOCATION	DATE/TIME

PELLITORY-OF-THE-WALL
Parietaria judaica

FACT FILE

SIZE Height to 70cm HABITAT Walls, cliffs, rocks,
dry hedge bottoms FLOWERING PERIOD Jun–Oct
HABIT Many-stemmed, sometimes sprawling perennial

IDENTIFICATION
Leaves are oval with a pointed tip; slightly
glossy dark green above, lighter below.
Flowers are tiny, green, in clusters against
stem. Fruits are tiny blobs at leaf base. Stems
are reddish, cylindrical, hairy. The plant may
have an overall reddish appearance.

KEY FACT

This close relative of the
Common Nettle is similar to that species
in some ways, but does not have stinging
hairs. Like the Common Nettle, it was
once widely used in herbal medicines.

STATUS AND COMMENTS
More common in the S and W, and often found near the sea. As its
name suggests, this plant is very much associated with walls and buildings,
especially those with crevices for
the roots.

SPOTTER'S CHART

LOCATION	DATE/TIME

BROAD-LEAVED DOCK
Rumex obtusifolius

FACT FILE

SIZE Height to 1m HABITAT Fields, hedges, waste ground, gardens FLOWERING PERIOD Jun–Aug HABIT Upright perennial

IDENTIFICATION

Leaves are up to 25cm long, oval, much broader than those of other dock species, and have a heart-shaped base. Flowers are tiny, reddish brown; in loose spikes. Fruits are in reddish-brown clusters. The entire plant may take on an attractive reddish-brown tinge at end of year.

STATUS AND COMMENTS

Common everywhere. It has a very similar, and equally common, relative in Curled Dock, but this has narrower leaves that are not heart-shaped at the base.

KEY FACT

Happily, docks often grow in the same places as Common Nettle, and their leaves can be rubbed onto stings from that plant to ease the pain.

SPOTTER'S CHART

LOCATION	DATE/TIME

WOOD DOCK
Rumex sanguineus

FACT FILE

SIZE **Height to 80cm** HABITAT **Woods, shaded fields**
FLOWERING PERIOD **Jun–Jul**
HABIT **Upright perennial**

IDENTIFICATION
Leaves are an elongated oval, lower ones heart-shaped at base; frequently red-veined. Flowers are tiny, in loose spikes. Fruits are in reddish-brown clusters. Overall, this plant is smaller in size and impact than Broad-leaved Dock, and is redder early in the year.

KEY FACT
Traditionally managed coppiced woodland is a good place to look for this plant. It thrives in the semi-shade.

STATUS AND COMMENTS
Although common, this species is less often noticed than other docks because of its preference for woods and woodland edges, and because of its modest appearance.

SPOTTER'S CHART

LOCATION	DATE/TIME

JAPANESE KNOTWEED
Fallopia japonica

FACT FILE

SIZE **Height to 2m** HABITAT **Waste ground, roadsides, hedgerows, gardens** FLOWERING PERIOD **Aug–Oct** HABIT **Large, upright perennial**

KEY FACT
Once established, Japanese Knotweed is notoriously difficult to eradicate. Even simply trying to keep it under control is often problematic.

IDENTIFICATION
Leaves are up to 14cm long; oval, with a blunt base. Flowers are white, very prominent; in loose, upright clusters all over plant. Stem is hollow, red-tinged, and grows in a distinct zigzag fashion. In some optimal growing conditions the plant can grow as much as 3m in one growing season.

STATUS AND COMMENTS
This is one of the world's most invasive plants, and is a real threat to native species, which it crowds out. Originally from Japan, it has become a pest everywhere it has been introduced.

SPOTTER'S CHART

LOCATION	DATE/TIME

PINK PURSLANE
Claytonia sibirica

SIZE **Height to 40cm** HABITAT **Damp woods, hedgerows, banks, verges, stream-sides** FLOWERING PERIOD **Apr–Jul** HABIT **Upright, rather fleshy annual or perennial**

IDENTIFICATION
Leaves are oval, pointed at tip and tapering at base, veined, glossy green; those at base of plant have stalks, those on stems do not. Flowers are bright pink, up to 20mm across, with five notched petals. Fruits are capsules.

KEY FACT Introduced from North America at least 200 years ago as a garden plant, Pink Purslane has since spread to many parts of Britain. It is an attractive species that sometimes grows in glossy drifts along ditched hedgerows and similar places.

STATUS AND COMMENTS
Pink Purslane is commonest in W Britain, but is also widespread elsewhere.

SPOTTER'S CHART

LOCATION	DATE/TIME

THREE-NERVED SANDWORT
Moehringia trinervia

SIZE Height to 40cm **HABITAT** Woodlands with rich soils **FLOWERING PERIOD** Apr–Jul **HABIT** Somewhat straggly, trailing annual

IDENTIFICATION
Leaves are oval, with three (sometimes five) conspicuous veins (the 'nerves') beneath. Flowers are white with five undivided petals (those of stitchworts and chickweeds are divided), held on longish upright stalks. Fruits are small brown seed capsules. Stem is red-tinged and wandering.

STATUS AND COMMENTS
Not uncommon, but easily overlooked. Its habitat of woodland clearings on rich soil helps to identify this modest little plant – it is the only sandwort found in woods.

KEY FACT

Ants are attracted to the oily seeds of this plant. They take them to their nests, thereby helping the plant to disperse.

SPOTTER'S CHART

LOCATION	DATE/TIME

GREATER STITCHWORT
Stellaria holostea

FACT FILE

SIZE **Height to 50cm** HABITAT **Woodlands, hedgerows, verges** FLOWERING PERIOD **Apr–Jun**
HABIT **Upright perennial**

IDENTIFICATION
Leaves are green, narrow and grass-like, with rough edges; carried in opposite pairs. Flowers are 20–25mm across with five notched white petals, carried on slender stems. Stem is square, rough-edged, very weak and easily broken.

KEY FACT Greater Stitchwort is so named because it was believed to alleviate the pain of a stitch in the side. The remedy was produced by mixing the plant with liquid and crushed acorns.

STATUS AND COMMENTS
Widespread and common throughout most of Britain, but absent from, or rare in, the Scottish Highlands and the far N and W.

SPOTTER'S CHART

LOCATION	DATE/TIME

LESSER STITCHWORT
Stellaria graminea

FACT FILE SIZE Height to 50cm HABITAT Woodlands,
hedgerows, heaths; prefers acid soils FLOWERING PERIOD May–Aug
HABIT Spreading, upright perennial

IDENTIFICATION
Leaves are slender and grass-like, with smooth edges (and smaller
than those of Greater Stitchwort). Flowers are white, with five deeply
divided petals (much smaller, and more deeply divided, than in Greater
Stitchwort). Stem is smooth-edged (rough-edged in Greater Stitchwort).

STATUS AND COMMENTS
Widespread and common
throughout most of Britain,
but absent from, or rare in, the
Scottish Highlands and the far
N and W.

KEY FACT
Even though it
is very similar to Greater
Stitchwort, and often grows
beside it, Lesser Stitchwort was
not traditionally used for any
medicinal purposes.

SPOTTER'S CHART

LOCATION	DATE/TIME

WOOD STITCHWORT
Stellaria nemorum

SIZE **Height to 60cm** HABITAT **Damp woodlands, wood edges** FLOWERING PERIOD **May–Aug** HABIT **Straggly perennial**

KEY FACT Perhaps the best way to find Wood Stitchwort is to look closely along the edges of damp woodland rides in late spring and summer when it is in flower.

IDENTIFICATION
Leaves are oval, pointed; lower leaves are stalked, upper ones unstalked. Flowers are white, up to 20mm across, with five very deeply divided petals (smaller than those of Greater Stitchwort). Stem is hairy. Straggly and wandering by nature, and easy to miss on the woodland floor.

SPOTTER'S CHART

LOCATION	DATE/TIME

STATUS AND COMMENTS
Not as common or as widespread as other stitchworts, Wood Stitchwort lives, as its name implies, in damp woodland; it is less common in the S and W.

FACT FILE

SIZE Height to 1m HABITAT Hedgerows, woods, field edges, cliffs FLOWERING PERIOD Mar–Oct
HABIT Upright biennial or perennial

IDENTIFICATION

Leaves are oval and appear in opposite pairs on stems; the larger, lower ones often stand out in the hedgerow. Flowers are dark pink, 20–30mm across; male and female flowers are produced on separate plants. Stem is softly hairy, with non-flowering shoots and upright flowering stems.

STATUS AND COMMENTS

Widespread and generally common in much of Britain, although absent from intensive farmland and uplands; often does extremely well near the coast.

KEY FACT

Red Campion flowers are not scented, unlike those of White Campion. When hybrids occur (which is often), the resulting pale pink flowers are also scented.

SPOTTER'S CHART

LOCATION	DATE/TIME

WHITE CAMPION
Silene latifolia

SIZE **Height to 1m** HABITAT **Meadows, grassy verges, disturbed ground** FLOWERING PERIOD **May–Oct** HABIT **Upright perennial**

IDENTIFICATION
Leaves are oval and appear in opposite pairs on stems. Flowers are white, fragrant, up to 30mm across (unscented and smaller in Red Campion); male and female flowers are produced on separate plants. Stem is hairy and slightly sticky. Often hybridises with Red Campion to create plants with flowers that range from deep pink to pure white.

KEY FACT
The flowers of White Campion are scented and attract moths in the evening, which pollinate them. Hybrids with Red Campion are also scented.

SPOTTER'S CHART

LOCATION	DATE/TIME

STATUS AND COMMENTS
Widespread and common throughout much of England and Wales, White Campion is more a plant of open ground than Red Campion, though the two often grow together.

FACT FILE

SIZE **Height to 80cm** HABITAT **Dry woodlands**
FLOWERING PERIOD **Jan–Apr**
HABIT **Large, dark-leaved perennial**

IDENTIFICATION

Leaves are palmate, with each leaflet toothed; lower, larger leaves are dark green; younger, smaller leaves are yellowish green. Flowers are yellowish green with purple-tinged tips; bell-shaped, in hanging clusters. The flowers attract early-flying bees, and the whole plant has a pungent aroma, which some find unpleasant.

STATUS AND COMMENTS

Not a common plant, and restricted to calcareous woodlands in S and central England. Insect larvae commonly known as leaf miners often create a pattern of unsightly brown squiggles on the leaves.

KEY FACT

The seeds exude an oil that attracts snails. The snails eat the oil and discard the seeds, which are thereby dispersed across the woodland floor.

SPOTTER'S CHART

LOCATION	DATE/TIME

GREEN HELLEBORE
Helleborus viridis

FACT FILE

SIZE Height to 60cm **HABITAT** Damp woodlands
FLOWERING PERIOD Feb–Apr
HABIT Upright perennial

IDENTIFICATION
Leaves are palmate, with each leaflet toothed; lower, larger leaves are dark green; younger, smaller leaves are lighter green. Flowers are green, spreading and open (unlike those of Stinking Hellebore; they also lack the purple tinge). Like Stinking Hellebore, this plant attracts bees.

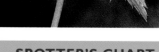

STATUS AND COMMENTS
This is a localised plant, most likely to be found in woods on limestone in S England, but also in some woods in Wales and central England.

KEY FACT
The leaves of Green Hellebore are deciduous, whereas the lower leaves of Stinking Hellebore persist through the winter. Green Hellebore has precise habitat requirements.

SPOTTER'S CHART

LOCATION	DATE/TIME

FACT FILE

SIZE **Height to 30cm** HABITAT **Woodlands, hedgerows** FLOWERING PERIOD **Mar–May** HABIT **Upright, creeping perennial**

KEY FACT On grey, sunless days Wood Anemone flowers stay closed, drooped and very inconspicuous, but as soon as the sun shines they stand up and open out fully, often transforming the woodland floor.

IDENTIFICATION

Leaves are palmately lobed, with groups of three-lobed leaflets on long stems. Flowers are very distinctive and familiar; white, often tinged pale pinkish purple; star-shaped. There is one per plant, these often forming extensive carpets.

STATUS AND COMMENTS

Found in woodlands throughout Britain, and sometimes creeping out into grassy meadows.

SPOTTER'S CHART	
LOCATION	DATE/TIME

WINTER ACONITE
Eranthis hyemalis

FACT FILE

SIZE **Height to 10cm** HABITAT **Woodlands, parks, gardens** FLOWERING PERIOD **Jan–Mar**
HABIT **Low perennial**

IDENTIFICATION
Leaves are palmate; they appear after flowers, except for a 'ruff' of small leaves immediately behind and with flower. Flowers are bright yellow, on longish stems. There is one flower per plant, these occasionally in carpets on the woodland floor, dying off as the trees come into leaf.

KEY FACT

Winter Aconite is a member of the buttercup family. Every part of the plant is poisonous.

STATUS AND COMMENTS
This native of S Europe was introduced to British gardens and has since escaped. It is quite common in some areas, especially in S England.

SPOTTER'S CHART

LOCATION	DATE/TIME

FACT FILE

SIZE **Height to 1m** HABITAT **Damp woodland, stream-sides** FLOWERING PERIOD **May–Aug** HABIT **Upright perennial**

IDENTIFICATION

Leaves are palmately lobed; lobes are thin and rounded at tip, and cut almost back to leaf base. Flowers are highly distinctive, dark blue or violet, up to 4cm across, with a pronounced hood; they grow in dense spikes. The plant is highly poisonous.

KEY FACT The *napellus* part of the species' scientific name means 'little turnip' and refers to the root, which is, in fact, deadly poisonous. There are several popular garden varieties of *Aconitum*.

STATUS AND COMMENTS

Native Monk's-hood (rather than similar escaped cultivated *Aconitum* species) is confined to damp woods and stream-sides in some parts of **SW England** and **Wales**. It is not common.

SPOTTER'S CHART

LOCATION	DATE/TIME

TRAVELLER'S-JOY
Clematis vitalba

SIZE Height to 30m **HABITAT** Woodlands, hedgerows, scrub **FLOWERING PERIOD** Jun–Aug
HABIT Very tall, scrambling, climbing perennial

IDENTIFICATION
Leaves are groups of three to five lanceolate leaflets on long stems; leaf stems curl around other plants to aid climbing. Flowers are creamy green, up to 2cm across, sweet-smelling. Fruits are clusters of seeds with feathery tufts, often produced in great profusion and conspicuous in winter. Mature stems can be very thick, fibrous and tough.

KEY FACT
A full-grown Traveller's-joy (or Old Man's Beard, as it is often known) can reach the top of a tall tree and have a free-hanging stem thicker than a man's wrist.

STATUS AND COMMENTS
A familiar sight on chalky and limy soils in much of **S Britain**.

SPOTTER'S CHART

LOCATION	DATE/TIME

FACT FILE SIZE **Height to 1m** HABITAT **Open woodland, scrub;**
usually on calcareous soils FLOWERING PERIOD **May–Jul**
HABIT **Upright perennial**

IDENTIFICATION

Leaves are of two sorts: lower leaves are in three parts, rounded and
deeply lobed; upper ones much smaller and simpler, but also in three
parts. Flowers are very
distinctive, usually dark blue
or purple, up to 5cm across,
drooping, with five petals
that have curling spurs.
Fruits are brown capsules
with small spikes.

KEY FACT

With its intriguing
nodding flowers, it is no wonder that
Columbine, or Aquilegia as it is also
known, is a firm garden favourite.
The species has hundreds of different
forms, colours and flower shapes.

STATUS AND COMMENTS

Native Columbine (rather than
escaped cultivated *Aquilegia*
species) can be found throughout
Britain as far N as S Scotland, but
it is not common.

SPOTTER'S CHART

LOCATION	DATE/TIME

GOLDILOCKS BUTTERCUP
Ranunculus auricomus

SIZE **Height to 30cm** HABITAT **Damp woodland, shady hedgerows** FLOWERING PERIOD **Apr–May** HABIT **Slender perennial**

IDENTIFICATION
Lowest leaves are rounded and only very slightly lobed; higher leaves are three-lobed; upper leaves are narrow. Flowers are yellow, often with parts of the petals missing or damaged, as if pecked by birds.

KEY FACT Goldilocks Buttercup has a more delicate, gentle appearance than other members of the buttercup family. It is the only buttercup of British woodlands.

STATUS AND COMMENTS
A widespread plant of British woodlands, but it requires undisturbed damp woods and is declining in many of its locations.

SPOTTER'S CHART

LOCATION	DATE/TIME

LESSER CELANDINE
Ranunculus ficaria

SIZE Height to 25cm **HABITAT** Woodland, hedgerows, waste ground **FLOWERING PERIOD** Mar–May **HABIT** Low-growing, creeping, patch-forming perennial

IDENTIFICATION
Leaves are heart-shaped, glossy, sometimes blotchy, dark green. Flowers are bright yellow; they open in sunshine, closing when it is cloudy or overcast. Fruiting body contains a single seed. The plant sometimes has bulbils (tiny bulbs) growing at the base of the leaf stem.

KEY FACT

Lesser Celandine is considered a nuisance by some when it makes carpets in gardens, but it is one of the brightest and most welcome of spring flowers.

STATUS AND COMMENTS
Dampish conditions suit the Lesser Celandine best, but it is common throughout Britain. In woodland it often flowers with Bluebells and Primroses. It tends to go unnoticed except when in flower.

SPOTTER'S CHART

LOCATION	DATE/TIME

GREATER CELANDINE
Chelidonium majus

SIZE Height to 90cm **HABITAT** Hedgerows, waste places, verges, walls **FLOWERING PERIOD** May–Aug
HABIT Upright, very leafy perennial

KEY FACT Possibly introduced to Britain, Greater Celandine is often found near houses, or where houses once were. The toxic sap can cause permanent and unsightly stains on clothing.

IDENTIFICATION
Leaves are pinnate; leaflets have rounded lobes, wrinkled; grey-green, often becoming rusty-looking. Flowers are bright yellow, up to 20mm across, with four well-spaced petals. Fruits are long, narrow capsules. Stems exude orange sap if broken; this is poisonous.

STATUS AND COMMENTS
Widespread throughout Britain, being commonest in the S and least common in N Scotland. It is a member of the poppy family.

SPOTTER'S CHART

LOCATION	DATE/TIME

FACT FILE

SIZE Height to 80cm
HABITAT Roadsides, hedgerows, field margins, waste ground
FLOWERING PERIOD May–Oct HABIT Upright annual or biennial

KEY FACT

This is a member of the mustard family, but it does not have the strong flavour of some of the other mustards, so has not been used much for culinary purposes in Britain.

IDENTIFICATION

Lower leaves are larger, deeply lobed and toothed, often with lower lobes pointing backwards; upper leaves are more narrow. Flowers are yellow, tiny, in small clusters at end of flowering stem. Fruits are cylindrical pods pressed close to stem. Stem is usually bristly.

STATUS AND COMMENTS

Widespread and locally common in central and S England, and in Wales; absent from uplands and much of N England; in Scotland, it is found mainly on the E coast.

SPOTTER'S CHART

LOCATION	DATE/TIME

GARLIC MUSTARD
Alliaria petiolata

SIZE Height to 1m HABITAT Waste places, hedgerows, woodland edges; prefers shelter
FLOWERING PERIOD Apr–Jun HABIT Upright biennial

IDENTIFICATION
Lower leaves are large, heart-shaped, toothed, shiny; upper ones are triangular. Flowers are white, small, four-petalled, in a group at top of plant. The plant smells of garlic, particularly the large lower leaves.

KEY FACT
Also known as Jack-by-the-hedge and Poor Man's Mustard, Garlic Mustard can be eaten, either raw or cooked. It is a foodplant of the Orange-tip butterfly.

STATUS AND COMMENTS
Widespread and common in much of England and Wales, but least so in N and upland areas; in Scotland, it is restricted mainly to the S and the E coast.

SPOTTER'S CHART

LOCATION	DATE/TIME

FACT FILE
SIZE **Height to 50cm** HABITAT **Damp places, including meadows, marshes, woodland rides and stream-sides** FLOWERING PERIOD **Apr–Jun** HABIT **Upright perennial**

IDENTIFICATION

Leaves are Watercress-like in shape; lower leaves are larger and form a rosette at base; leaves on flowering stem are smaller. Flowers range from deep pink through pale pink to white, sometimes double; 14–20mm across with four petals. Fruits are thin pods held against stem. Stem is hairless and erect.

KEY FACT This is one of those very attractive, well-loved country flowers with many charming local names, including Milkmaids and Lady's Smock. It is a foodplant of the Orange-tip butterfly.

STATUS AND COMMENTS

Widespread and locally common in suitable habitats throughout much of England and Wales; widespread in Scotland, although absent from harsh uplands.

SPOTTER'S CHART

LOCATION	DATE/TIME

CORALROOT BITTERCRESS
Cardamine bulbifera

SIZE **Height to 70cm** HABITAT **Very localised:
chalky or sandy woods** FLOWERING PERIOD **Apr–Jun**
HABIT **Upright perennial**

IDENTIFICATION
Leaves are on stem; lower leaves are larger and comprise three spear-shaped, toothed leaflets; upper ones are much smaller and single. Flowers are lilac to purple; small, in loose clusters at top of plant. Fruits are often small bulbils at base of upper leaves. Stem is thin, hairless and erect.

STATUS AND COMMENTS
An uncommon plant, restricted to dry woodlands in the S. It is distinguishable from Cuckooflower and other bittercresses by its habitat, leaf shape and absence of basal leaves.

KEY FACT

Coralroot (as it is often simply known) takes its name from the strange thick, fleshy white scales that cover the creeping rootstock.

SPOTTER'S CHART

LOCATION	DATE/TIME

OPPOSITE-LEAVED GOLDEN SAXIFRAGE
Chrysosplenium oppositifolium

FACT FILE
SIZE **Height to 15cm** HABITAT **Wet, shady woodlands, stream-sides, among rocks** FLOWERING PERIOD **Apr–Jul** HABIT **Low, mat-forming perennial**

KEY FACT
Closely related and very similar is Alternate-leaved Golden Saxifrage, whose name helps to identify it: the leaves are alternate on the stem, and it has no leafy creeping stems.

IDENTIFICATION
Leaves are rounded with blunt teeth, in opposite pairs, pale green. Flowers are tiny, golden, in small groups on an upright stem carried above a sprawling mat of leaves that includes leafy creeping stems.

STATUS AND COMMENTS
This plant has very particular habitat requirements. It can be found throughout Britain in suitable damp places.

SPOTTER'S CHART

LOCATION	DATE/TIME

RASPBERRY
Rubus idaeus

SIZE **Height to 1.5m** HABITAT **Woods, wasteland, thick hedges, banks** FLOWERING PERIOD **May–Aug** HABIT **Upright perennial**

IDENTIFICATION
Leaves are pinnate, with three to seven toothed leaflets; downy beneath. Flowers are white with five petals; small (1cm across) and inconspicuous. Fruit is the familiar raspberry; red when ripe. New stems are sent up each year from the rootstock; they fruit the following year.

KEY FACT
Garden varieties of Raspberry have bigger fruits, but the original 'wild' Raspberry has equally edible fruits, which were long enjoyed in preserves and wines, and as a medicine.

STATUS AND COMMENTS
A common plant throughout much of Britain, probably often disregarded as being a garden escape, but actually a native species.

SPOTTER'S CHART

LOCATION	DATE/TIME

FACT FILE

SIZE **Height to 1m** HABITAT **Woods, wasteland,** hedgerows; also a garden escape FLOWERING PERIOD **Mar–May** HABIT **Small, untidy perennial**

IDENTIFICATION

Leaves are rounded, irregularly lobed, toothed. Flowers are greenish yellow with purple edges, small (1cm across) and inconspicuous, in little clusters. Fruit is the familiar hairy green gooseberry. Has sharp spines on stem at leaf bases.

KEY FACT As with Raspberries, wild Gooseberries were enjoyed for centuries but were supplanted in gardens by the introduction of cultivated forms with bigger fruits.

STATUS AND COMMENTS

Common through much of Britain, both as a native plant and as one that has escaped from cultivation and become naturalised.

SPOTTER'S CHART

LOCATION	DATE/TIME

BLACK CURRANT
Ribes nigrum

SIZE Height to 2m **HABITAT** Woods, hedgerows, fens; also a garden escape **FLOWERING PERIOD** Apr–May **HABIT** Upright perennial

IDENTIFICATION

Leaves are rounded, irregularly lobed, toothed, slightly sticky; aromatic when rubbed (Red Currant leaves have no aroma). Flowers are greenish with purple tips to petals; in small, hanging clusters. Fruit is the well-known currant, black when ripe.

KEY FACT
This is the familiar garden 'soft fruit', long cultivated and used in preserves. Many would argue that Black Currants make more useful and longer-lasting preserves than Red Currants.

STATUS AND COMMENTS

Locally common as a native plant, Black Currant is also a regular garden escapee. Native Black Currant prefers damp or wet habitats.

SPOTTER'S CHART

LOCATION	DATE/TIME

FACT FILE

SIZE **Height to 1.5m** HABITAT **Woods, hedgerows; also a garden escape** FLOWERING PERIOD **Apr–May** HABIT **Untidy perennial**

IDENTIFICATION

Leaves are rounded, irregularly lobed, toothed, slightly downy; no aroma (Black Currant leaves are aromatic when rubbed). Flowers are greenish; in hanging clusters, with up to twice as many in each cluster as Black Currant. Fruit is the well-known currant, red when ripe.

STATUS AND COMMENTS

More widespread and common as a native plant than Black Currant, Red Currant is also a regular garden escapee. Native Red Currant thrives in even wetter habitats than Black Currant.

KEY FACT

This is another familiar garden 'soft fruit', long cultivated and used in preserves, and perhaps best known in red currant jelly. Birds love Red Currants rather more than Black Currants.

SPOTTER'S CHART

LOCATION	DATE/TIME

BARREN STRAWBERRY
Potentilla sterilis

FACT FILE

SIZE Height to 15cm HABITAT Woods, hedgerows, dry banks FLOWERING PERIOD Mar–May HABIT Low, creeping perennial

IDENTIFICATION
Leaves comprise three leaflets, these rounded, toothed, with the topmost tooth lower than those on either side; dull, bluish green. Flowers are white, with prominent gaps between the five petals, through which the sepals beneath are clearly visible. Fruits are papery and dry, never becoming strawberries.

KEY FACT Barren Strawberry and Wild Strawberry are easily confused, but Barren Strawberry has no juicy fruits, has duller leaves with blunter tips, and has flowers with much more widely spaced petals.

STATUS AND COMMENTS
A common plant of dry, grassy places, including woodland rides. It can be found throughout Britain apart from the N tip of Scotland.

SPOTTER'S CHART

LOCATION	DATE/TIME

FACT FILE

SIZE **Height to 20cm** HABITAT **Woods, hedgerows, grassy banks** FLOWERING PERIOD **Apr–Jul** HABIT **Low, creeping perennial**

IDENTIFICATION

Leaves have three leaflets, these rounded, toothed, with the topmost tooth higher than those on either side; hairy beneath and bright, glossy green above; on long stems. Flowers are white, with only small gaps between the five petals. Fruits are small, edible strawberries.

KEY FACT The Alpine Strawberry is a form of the Wild Strawberry selected for bigger, juicier fruits. Garden Strawberries are a hybrid first raised in France in the 18th century.

STATUS AND COMMENTS

Very common throughout Britain, particularly on dry, grassy banks, waysides and woodland edges. To be palatable, the little fruits need to be completely red and ripe.

SPOTTER'S CHART

LOCATION	DATE/TIME

BRAMBLE
Rubus fruticosus

FACT FILE

SIZE **Height to 3m** HABITAT **Woods, hedgerows, wasteland, forgotten corners** FLOWERING PERIOD **May–Aug** HABIT **Vigorous, spreading shrub with arching stems**

IDENTIFICATION
Leaves are divided into three to four toothed leaflets. Flowers are white, occasionally pink. Fruit is the blackberry – surely the most well-known of all hedgerow foods. Blackberries begin red, ripening to shiny black; they become fly-blown and unpalatable with age.

KEY FACT
The name of this familiar hedgerow fruit differs between the N and the S. In N England and Scotland it is often called Bramble, while in the S it is almost always called Blackberry.

STATUS AND COMMENTS
Common throughout Britain, the Bramble is a plant with a complex family background and several thousand subspecies. This accounts for the variable leaf shapes, sharpness of prickles, etc.

SPOTTER'S CHART

LOCATION	DATE/TIME

FACT FILE

SIZE **Height to 20cm** HABITAT **Damp woodlands, hedgerows, scrub** FLOWERING PERIOD **May–Sep**
HABIT **Low-growing, sprawling shrub, with creeping stems**

KEY FACT

In comparison to Bramble, Dewberry is an altogether less prepossessing plant: much smaller, weaker, and with mealy (though blackberry-like) fruits that do not invite eating.

IDENTIFICATION

Leaves comprise three oblong, toothed leaflets. Flowers are always white. Fruits are rather like blackberries but always with an unpalatable-looking, waxy bluish bloom and far fewer, but larger, segments. Stems are weak in comparison to those of Bramble, and less prickly.

SPOTTER'S CHART

LOCATION	DATE/TIME

STATUS AND COMMENTS

Locally common throughout England and Wales, but less so in Scotland. It can tolerate damper soils than Bramble.

ORPINE
Sedum telephium

FACT FILE

SIZE **Height to 50cm** HABITAT **Shady woodland, thick hedgerows** FLOWERING PERIOD **Jul–Sep** HABIT **Tall, imposing perennial**

IDENTIFICATION
Leaves are flat, oval, fleshy (they store water), toothed. Flowers are deep pinkish purple with five petals, in conspicuous flattish heads; very prominent and distinctive. Fruits are purple, oval; do not open out when ripe. Stems are frequently reddish. It shines out from the shady areas that it prefers.

KEY FACT Orpine looks more like a garden plant than a wild one because some of its relatives are garden favourites. It may look exotic but is actually native to Britain.

STATUS AND COMMENTS
Locally common throughout Britain, but less so in N Scotland. It is unlikely to be mistaken for anything else in the countryside.

SPOTTER'S CHART

LOCATION	DATE/TIME

SIZE **Height to 50cm** HABITAT **Grassy banks, hedgerows, roadsides, field edges** FLOWERING PERIOD **Jun–Aug** HABIT **Upright perennial**

KEY FACT

Agrimony makes its presence felt in high summer, when the flowering spike is very apparent. The species' distinctive looks account for such country names as Aaron's Rod and Fairy's Wand.

IDENTIFICATION

Leaves are pinnate, with individual leaflets becoming bigger towards tip of leaf; between the larger leaflets are very much smaller leaflets. Flowers are yellow, small (up to 8mm across) and numerous on single, stiff stem. Fruits are small and brown, with tiny hooked bristles; they disperse by catching on passing animals (and people).

STATUS AND COMMENTS

Widespread and locally common in suitable habitats across much of central and S England; restricted mostly to lowland areas in Wales, N England and S Scotland.

SPOTTER'S CHART

LOCATION	DATE/TIME

DOG ROSE
Rosa canina

FACT FILE

SIZE **Height to 3m** HABITAT **Roadsides, hedgerows, wood edges** FLOWERING PERIOD **Jun–Jul**
HABIT **Vigorous, clambering shrub with long, arching stems**

IDENTIFICATION
Leaves have five to seven toothed leaflets that may be hairy or hairless; very variable. Flowers are pink (or white) with five petals, in clusters of up to four flowers. Fruits are oval red 'hips' that shed their sepals before ripening. Whole plant has curved thorns.

KEY FACT
Dog Rose may be Britain's most common wild rose, but it can be all but impossible to tell it reliably from some other wild roses, especially as they hybridise and because Dog Rose itself has 60 or so different known forms.

SPOTTER'S CHART

LOCATION	DATE/TIME

STATUS AND COMMENTS
Britain's most common and widespread wild rose, although it is not so common in Scotland. It is an ancestor of the myriad forms and types of garden rose, and is also the source of rose-hip syrup.

SIZE **Height to 1m** HABITAT **Woodland, hedgerows, scrub; prefers heavy soils** FLOWERING PERIOD **Jul–Aug** HABIT **Low, scrambling shrub**

Field Rose rarely hybridises, so its differences from Dog Rose should be a clear aid to identification: it is smaller and always has white flowers, and the hips are more rounded.

IDENTIFICATION

Leaves have five to seven leaflets, these oval, toothed and hairless. Flowers are white (never pink), cup-shaped, up to 50mm across, and carried in clusters of up to six. Fruits are rounded red hips; sepals fall off before hip ripens. Stem is weak, trailing, reddish, with curved thorns.

SPOTTER'S CHART

LOCATION	DATE/TIME

STATUS AND COMMENTS

A common plant throughout England and Wales, but absent from Scotland. Despite its name, it is most often found in or close to woodland.

SWEET BRIAR
Rosa rubiginosa

FACT FILE

SIZE Height to 2m **HABITAT** Hedgerows, grassland; usually on calcareous soils **FLOWERING PERIOD** Jun–Jul **HABIT** Shrub

KEY FACT This is the Eglantine mentioned in Shakespeare's plays, and is most easily told from other wild roses by its very distinctive sweet, apple-like scent.

IDENTIFICATION
Leaves have five to seven leaflets, these small, oval to round, toothed and sweetly scented. Flowers are pink, up to 30mm across, and carried in clusters of up to three. Fruits are oval red hips; sepals remain on ripe hips. Leaf stalk and sepals are covered in sticky, scented hairs.

STATUS AND COMMENTS
Much less common than Dog Rose or Field Rose, Sweet Briar is found locally in England and Wales, most often on limestone or chalk; it is rare in Scotland.

SPOTTER'S CHART

LOCATION	DATE/TIME

FACT FILE

SIZE **Height to 2m** HABITAT **Hedgerows, woodland edges, scrub, grassy banks** FLOWERING PERIOD **Jun–Jul** HABIT **Large, vigorous shrub with arching stems**

KEY FACT The downy leaflets are a good way of telling this species from other wild roses. The very similar Soft Downy Rose has a more upright habit, and is more likely to retain the sepals on its hips.

IDENTIFICATION

Leaves have five to seven leaflets, these oval, toothed and very downy, as the plant's name suggests. Flowers are pink or white, up to 40mm across, and borne in clusters of up to five. Fruits are oval red hips. Stems have thorns that are straighter than those of other wild roses, but not as straight as on Soft Downy Rose.

STATUS AND COMMENTS

Also known as Harsh Downy Rose, Downy Rose is fairly common in S England and in Wales, but rare in Scotland. In N England, Soft Downy Rose is more likely to be found.

SPOTTER'S CHART

LOCATION	DATE/TIME

WOOD AVENS
Geum urbanum

FACT FILE

SIZE **Height to 60cm** HABITAT **Open woodland,
hedgerows, scrub, grassy banks** FLOWERING PERIOD **May–Sep**
HABIT **Distinctive upright perennial**

IDENTIFICATION
Lower leaves are larger, pinnate, with rounded, toothed leaflets, the
terminal one being largest; upper leaves are smaller, with three leaflets.
Flowers are bright yellow with five petals, behind which are longer sepals;
borne at end of long stem. Fruits
are tiny and round, with long
hooks that catch on passing
animals for dispersal.

STATUS AND COMMENTS
Found throughout Britain, and
despite its common name is not
confined to woods. It prefers shade
and shelter, but can also make its
way into less likely places such as
flower borders.

KEY FACT

The cheerful
little yellow flowers and bold
green leaves help to identify this
plant. Its common country name
of Herb Bennet in part tells of
its use as a cottage herb; its root
kept the Devil away.

SPOTTER'S CHART

LOCATION	DATE/TIME

FACT FILE SIZE Height to 50cm HABITAT Damp woodlands in the W and in Wales; also in gardens FLOWERING PERIOD Jun–Aug HABIT Delicate, feathery-looking perennial

IDENTIFICATION

Leaves are pinnate, with deeply lobed leaflets, these rounded to heart-shaped and often overlapping their neighbours; lower leaves are on longer stems. Flowers are bright yellow, up to 4cm across, with five petals; borne at end of long stem. Seed capsules are up to 2.5cm long, with slits through which seeds disperse.

STATUS AND COMMENTS

Welsh Poppy was first identified in Wales, but it is also native to parts of the West Country. It is the only *Meconopsis* poppy found growing wild in Europe, and is also widely grown in gardens.

KEY FACT

Welsh Poppy differs in many ways from other poppies found in Britain, not least because its seedpod does not have the 'pepper pot' seed dispenser at the top, but vertical slits instead.

SPOTTER'S CHART

LOCATION	DATE/TIME

BROOM
Cytisus scoparius

SIZE Height to 2m **HABITAT** Heaths, cliffs, hedgerows, roadsides, waste places **FLOWERING PERIOD** Apr–Jul **HABIT** Tall, many-branched deciduous shrub

KEY FACT
Broom really was used as a sweeping implement, its long, whippy branches being tied together for the purpose. Country people considered it a magic plant from which the fairies spoke.

IDENTIFICATION
Leaves comprise three oval leaflets on a long stalk. Flowers are bright yellow, up to 2cm across, pea-like. Seedpods are pea-like, ripening to black; on hot, sunny days the ripe pods explode, ejecting small black seeds. When in full flower, the entire plant is cloaked in yellow blooms.

SPOTTER'S CHART

LOCATION	DATE/TIME

STATUS AND COMMENTS
Common throughout Britain, but generally confined to acid soils. Usually it is tall and upright, but it can be prostrate when growing on exposed cliffs.

FACT FILE SIZE Height to 2m HABITAT Moors, heaths, cliffs, waste places FLOWERING PERIOD Year-round, but at its best Apr–May HABIT Often a dome-shaped evergreen shrub

IDENTIFICATION
Leaves of young plants have three leaflets, while those of adult plants are long green spines. Flowers are bright yellow, up to 2cm long, pea-like, sweetly scented. Seedpods are brown and pea-like; on hot, sunny days the ripe pods explode, ejecting the seeds. The entire plant is very spiny.

STATUS AND COMMENTS
Common throughout Britain, usually on acid soils. If grazed, it can be reduced to small, very spiny, rounded hummocks.

KEY FACT
There are two other gorses in Britain: Western Gorse, which is found mainly in the W; and Dwarf Gorse, which is mostly restricted to heaths in the SE and E.

SPOTTER'S CHART

LOCATION	DATE/TIME

RIBBED MELILOT
Melilotus officinalis

SIZE Height to 1.25m **HABITAT** Grassy banks, waste places, roadsides **FLOWERING PERIOD** Jun–Sep **HABIT** Upright biennial

IDENTIFICATION
Leaves comprise three oblong, toothed leaflets on stalks. Flowers are bright yellow, pea-like, in showy spikes up to 6cm long. Fruits are ribbed brown pods. The leaves and stems smell sweetly of new-mown hay (they contain coumarin, a chemical that also makes some grasses aromatic).

STATUS AND COMMENTS
Widespread and common in central England; coastal and largely absent inland in SW England, Wales and N England; restricted to S lowlands in Scotland.

KEY FACT
There are several other melilots in Britain, including White Melilot, with white flowers, and Tall or Golden Melilot, which is very similar to Ribbed Melilot but has smooth (not ribbed) black seedpods.

SPOTTER'S CHART

LOCATION	DATE/TIME

FACT FILE

SIZE **Height to 2m** HABITAT **Grassy banks, hedgerows, woodland edges, waste places, roadsides** FLOWERING PERIOD **Jun–Aug** HABIT **Scrambling perennial**

IDENTIFICATION

Leaves comprise up to 12 pairs of lanceolate leaflets; at end of leaf stem is a branched, twining tendril. Flowers are purplish blue, up to 12mm long, carried in prominent one-sided spikes. Fruits are smooth, blunt-ended brown pods. The plant often has numerous close-knit, twining stems.

KEY FACT

Of Britain's vetches, this is one of the most common, distinguishable by its bright, dense flower spikes; most other vetches have looser, duller flowers.

STATUS AND COMMENTS

Common throughout Britain (though not so widespread in N Scotland), Tufted Vetch is sometimes grown in gardens for its striking flowers.

SPOTTER'S CHART

LOCATION	DATE/TIME

BUSH VETCH
Vicia sepium

SIZE **Height to 1m** HABITAT **Grassy banks, scrub and woodland edges** FLOWERING PERIOD **May–Aug** HABIT **Medium-tall, twining perennial**

IDENTIFICATION
Leaves comprise up to 12 pairs of oval leaflets; at end of leaf stem is a branched, twining tendril. Flowers are pale lilac, up to 15mm long, in groups of up to six. Fruits are black pods, tapered at beak.

KEY FACT Differences in the pods help to identify some of the vetches: Bush Vetch has black pods, whereas Tufted Vetch has brown; the black pods of Wood Vetch are tapered at both ends.

STATUS AND COMMENTS
Common and widespread throughout Britain, Bush Vetch is more likely to be found in rough, grassy places, and can be a garden weed.

SPOTTER'S CHART

LOCATION	DATE/TIME

FACT FILE SIZE **Height to 70cm** HABITAT **Hedgerows, grassy banks, pasture, waste ground** FLOWERING PERIOD **Apr–Sep** HABIT **Scrambling annual**

IDENTIFICATION

Leaves comprise up to eight pairs of variable leaflets, these narrow or oval; at end of leaf stem is a branched tendril; stipules at base of each leaf stem often have a black dot. Flowers are deep pink, up to 2.5cm long, usually single or in pairs. Fruits are variable black or brown pods.

KEY FACT

Common Vetch is native to Britain. However, its true wild distribution is hard to determine because it was once widely cultivated and relict populations linger on.

STATUS AND COMMENTS

Widespread and generally common in lowland England and Wales; more local in Scotland, where it is absent from the Highlands and far N and W.

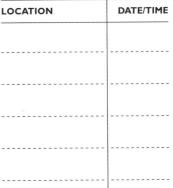

SPOTTER'S CHART

LOCATION	DATE/TIME

WOOD VETCH
Vicia sylvatica

FACT FILE

SIZE **Height to 1.5m** HABITAT **Open woodland, wood edges, sometimes on sea cliffs and shingle**
FLOWERING PERIOD **Jun–Aug** HABIT **Climbing perennial**

KEY FACT
Wood Vetch can be told from some other vetches by its large, elegant, purple-veined flowers. Wood Bitter-vetch has very similar flowers, but it does not have twining tendrils.

IDENTIFICATION
Leaves comprise up to 12 pairs of oblong leaflets; at end of leaf stem is a branched, twining tendril. Flowers are white or very pale lilac with purple veins, up to 20mm long, borne in groups of up to 20. Fruits are black pods, tapered at both ends.

STATUS AND COMMENTS
Wood Vetch has an idiosyncratic, localised distribution: it is found in some woods, but it can also sometimes be found by the sea, in shingle (where it may be stunted) and on cliffs.

SPOTTER'S CHART

LOCATION	DATE/TIME

SQUARE-STALKED ST JOHN'S-WORT
Hypericum tetrapterum

FACT FILE

SIZE Height to 90cm **HABITAT** Woodland paths, marshy grassland; prefers damp soils **FLOWERING PERIOD** Jun–Sep **HABIT** Upright perennial

IDENTIFICATION

Leaves are oval and have pale dots that are translucent when viewed against the light. Flowers are glossy yellow, five-petalled, up to 20mm across; in loose heads at end of stems. Fruits are dry capsules. Stem is square, with four distinct narrow wings running the entire length.

KEY FACT

The St John's-worts are very similar in appearance, but Square-stalked St John's-wort is true to its name, with its very distinctive ribbed stems. Its preference for damp habitats is a further clue to its identity.

STATUS AND COMMENTS

Widespread and locally common in England and Wales, and least numerous on dry ground and in upland districts; in Scotland, widespread and fairly common only in the S and SW.

SPOTTER'S CHART

LOCATION	DATE/TIME

PERFORATE ST JOHN'S-WORT
Hypericum perforatum

FACT FILE

SIZE **Height to 75cm** HABITAT **Grassy places, scrub, woodland rides and edges; prefers chalky soils**
FLOWERING PERIOD **Jun–Sep** HABIT **Upright perennial**

IDENTIFICATION
Leaves are oval and have pale spots that are translucent when seen against the light. Flowers are rich yellow, five-petalled, up to 20mm across; sometimes with dark spots on petal margins. Fruits are dry capsule. Stem is round, with two distinct narrow ridges running the entire length.

KEY FACT
The name of this St John's-wort helps to identify it: if it is held up to the light, tiny translucent glands, resembling perforations, are visible on the leaves; the very similar Imperforate St John's-wort does not have these.

SPOTTER'S CHART

LOCATION	DATE/TIME

STATUS AND COMMENTS
Widespread and locally common in England and Wales, least numerous in the N and usually absent from acid soils; in Scotland, restricted to lowlands in the S and E.

IMPERFORATE ST JOHN'S-WORT
Hypericum maculatum

SIZE **Height to 85cm** HABITAT **Scrub, woodland rides and edges; prefers shade and heavier soils** FLOWERING PERIOD **Jun–Aug** HABIT **Upright perennial**

IDENTIFICATION

Leaves are oval and do not have pale, translucent dots when viewed against the light. Flowers are yellow, five-petalled, up to 20mm across, with black dots on petal margins. Fruits are dry capsules. Stem is square in cross section.

STATUS AND COMMENTS

This St John's-wort is not quite so common or widespread as others, and prefers more shady situations on heavier soils than Perforate St John's-wort.

KEY FACT

To distinguish Imperforate St John's-wort from its Perforate cousin, look at the stem profile (square in the former, rounded in the latter) and the leaves (translucent dots absent in the former, present in the latter).

SPOTTER'S CHART

LOCATION	DATE/TIME

WOOD SORREL
Oxalis acetosella

FACT FILE

SIZE Height to 15cm HABITAT Woodlands, hedgerows FLOWERING PERIOD Apr–Jun HABIT Low, creeping perennial

KEY FACT
Like its leaves, the flowers of Wood Sorrel close in wet weather and at night. The spring flowers are followed by inconspicuous, non-opening summer flowers that self-pollinate.

IDENTIFICATION
Leaves comprise three heart-shaped leaflets at the end of a long stem; leaflets fold down on stem in poor weather and at night. Flowers are on long stalks, white, with five petals that have lilac veins.

STATUS AND COMMENTS
Common throughout Britain in dry woods, Wood Sorrel is a pretty little plant with several cultivated relatives.

SPOTTER'S CHART

LOCATION	DATE/TIME

SIZE **Height to 75cm** HABITAT **Grassy verges, meadows, field edges** FLOWERING PERIOD **Jun–Sep** HABIT **Upright, clump-forming, hairy perennial**

IDENTIFICATION
Leaves are up to 15cm across, divided into up to seven very deeply lobed sections that are markedly toothed; large lower leaves are on long stems rising from base. Flowers are striking, violet to blue, up to 3cm across, with five veined petals. Fruits are beaked seed capsules.

STATUS AND COMMENTS
Locally common throughout Britain, but uncommon in SE England and N Scotland. It prefers calcareous soils.

SPOTTER'S CHART

LOCATION	DATE/TIME

KEY FACT
The large, attractive flowers of Meadow Crane's-bill make it stand out on banks on country lanes. Many cultivated forms are grown in gardens, from which they sometimes escape.

WOOD CRANE'S-BILL
Geranium sylvaticum

SIZE Height to 60cm **HABITAT** Open woodlands, damp meadows **FLOWERING PERIOD** Jun–Sep **HABIT** Upright perennial

IDENTIFICATION
Leaves are divided into up to seven deeply lobed sections with rounded teeth (more rounded than on Meadow Crane's-bill). Flowers are reddish purple, up to 2.5cm across, cup-shaped, with five veined petals; held upright on stem. Fruits are beaked seed capsules.

STATUS AND COMMENTS
Quite common in N England. It is rarer elsewhere, including Wales, and is absent from S and SW England. It prefers damp, upland habitats.

KEY FACT
The species' distribution and flower colour will often help to distinguish it from Meadow Crane's-bill. A further clue is its upright flowers: those of Meadow Crane's-bill are on drooping stems.

SPOTTER'S CHART

LOCATION	DATE/TIME

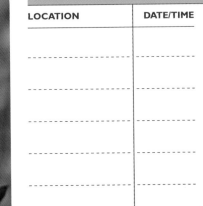

HEDGEROW CRANE'S-BILL
Geranium pyrenaicum

FACT FILE

SIZE **Height to 60cm** HABITAT **Roadsides, grassy banks, scrub, open woodland** FLOWERING PERIOD **Jun–Sep** HABIT **Upright, hairy perennial**

IDENTIFICATION

Leaves are rounded overall (not nearly as incised as in Meadow or Wood Crane's-bills), and divided into up to seven lobed sections with rounded teeth. Flowers are deep pink, up to 15mm across, with five deeply notched petals; borne in pairs. Fruits are beaked seed capsules.

STATUS AND COMMENTS

It is possible that this plant was introduced from Europe. It is locally common in S England, but less widespread and less common throughout the rest of Britain.

KEY FACT

The species could be confused with the very common Dove's-foot Crane's-bill, but that is much smaller – only up to 20cm tall, with tiny flowers – and prefers drier, grassy habitats.

SPOTTER'S CHART

LOCATION	DATE/TIME

HERB-ROBERT
Geranium robertianum

FACT FILE

SIZE **Height to 30cm** HABITAT **Roadsides, woodland, waste places, shingle, rocks** FLOWERING PERIOD **Apr–Nov** HABIT **Short, straggling, hairy annual**

IDENTIFICATION
Leaves are broadly triangular, divided into three or five deeply lobed sections with deep, rounded teeth. Flowers are pink, up to 15mm across, with five well-spaced petals; pollen is orange. Fruits are hairy, beaked seed capsules. The whole plant is often red-tinged and has a distinctive sharp scent that some find unpleasant.

KEY FACT
This tough little plant is very closely related to the many different perennial geraniums that gardeners tend so carefully. Its white form is cultivated as a cottage garden plant. The leaves of Herb-Robert often turn an intense red in the autumn.

STATUS AND COMMENTS
Common and widespread throughout Britain: found from woods to shores, and woodlands to grassland. It seeds abundantly and is often found as a garden weed.

SPOTTER'S CHART

LOCATION	DATE/TIME

SHINING CRANE'S-BILL
Geranium lucidum

FACT FILE SIZE Height to 30cm HABITAT Grassy banks, hedgerows, rocks, walls; prefers shade FLOWERING PERIOD May–Aug HABIT Upright, branched, hairless annual

IDENTIFICATION
Leaves are shiny, rounded, divided into five or seven lobed sections with two or three blunt teeth, and borne on long stalks. Flowers are pink, up to 10mm across, with five unnotched petals. Fruits are beaked seed capsules. The plant is often red-tinged.

KEY FACT This plant might be confused with Herb-Robert because both tend to become red, but Herb-Robert has much more deeply divided leaves and is much less fussy about its location.

STATUS AND COMMENTS
Widespread in Britain, but less common in some areas than others. It has a preference for shady locations on limestone soils.

SPOTTER'S CHART

LOCATION	DATE/TIME

WOOD SPURGE
Euphorbia amygdaloides

FACT FILE

SIZE Height to 80cm **HABITAT** Woodland, scrub
FLOWERING PERIOD Apr–Jun
HABIT Upright, unbranched perennial

IDENTIFICATION
Leaves are lanceolate, short-stalked, downy, up to 8cm long. Flowers are very unusual in structure and looks: yellow-green, cup-shaped, lacking petals and sepals; upper bracts look rather like petals at first sight. Fruits are rounded capsules. Plants are often red-tinged.

KEY FACT Wood Spurge has many wild and garden relatives, including Sun Spurge and Petty Spurge, both of which are smaller annual plants found in open, disturbed or cultivated soils.

STATUS AND COMMENTS
Common in woodlands in S England and Wales, but rare or absent in other parts of Britain. Spurges contain poisons that can be lethal if ingested and their sap often causes skin inflammation.

SPOTTER'S CHART

LOCATION	DATE/TIME

DOG'S MERCURY
Mercurialis perennis

SIZE **Height to 40cm** HABITAT **Woodland, scrub, hedgerows, banks** FLOWERING PERIOD **Feb–Apr** HABIT **Upright perennial**

IDENTIFICATION

Leaves are shiny, oval with a pointed tip, toothed. Flowers are tiny, yellow, borne in long, upward-growing, slender spikes; male and female flowers are on separate plants. Fruits are small, hairy balls. Often one of the commonest plants on woodland floors.

KEY FACT The similar Annual Mercury is an annual plant of cultivated land and waste ground; it is not hairy, is branched and is bigger. Both Dog's Mercury and Annual Mercury are poisonous.

STATUS AND COMMENTS

Common throughout much of Britain, but absent from, or rare in, N Scotland. Dog's Mercury is sometimes found on shady mountain slopes.

SPOTTER'S CHART

LOCATION	DATE/TIME

COMMON MALLOW
Malva sylvestris

SIZE Height to 1.25m **HABITAT** Roadsides, waste
ground, grassy places; prefers dry conditions
FLOWERING PERIOD Jun–Oct **HABIT** Upright perennial

IDENTIFICATION
Leaves are palmately lobed, toothed, wrinkled; those at base are more
rounded. Flowers are large and showy (up to 4cm across), borne in
clusters; pink with dark veins and five notched petals. Fruits are distinctive
flat, rounded capsules, often described as 'buttons' or 'cheeses'.

STATUS AND COMMENTS
Common and widespread
throughout much of Britain,
especially the S, but rarer or
absent in N Scotland. Its fruits
have lent it many country names,
including **Billy Buttons**.

KEY FACT

The similar
Musk Mallow is smaller, with
smaller, paler flowers, and has
deeply divided leaves on the
stems that are very different
from those of **Common Mallow**.

SPOTTER'S CHART

LOCATION	DATE/TIME

FACT FILE

SIZE Height to 15cm HABITAT Woodland, scrub, hedgerows, banks FLOWERING PERIOD Feb–May HABIT Low, creeping perennial

IDENTIFICATION
Leaves are glossy, rounded, veined, becoming heart-shaped and larger in summer; stalks arise from a basal rosette. Flowers are scented, usually violet or white, up to 15mm across. Fruits are hairy, rounded capsules. The key identifier is the scented flowers; no other violets are scented.

KEY FACT The lovely scent of Sweet Violet is elusive: once you have sniffed it, it disappears for a while, along with other scents. After a while your sense of smell returns, until you sniff the flower again.

STATUS AND COMMENTS
Common throughout Britain, but rarer in Scotland. Although flowers are most commonly violet and white in colour, lilacs, pinks and even yellows can be encountered.

SPOTTER'S CHART

LOCATION	DATE/TIME

COMMON DOG-VIOLET
Viola riviniana

FACT FILE

SIZE Height to 12cm **HABITAT** Woodland, scrub, hedgerows, grassy banks **FLOWERING PERIOD** Mar–May
HABIT Low perennial

IDENTIFICATION
Leaves are glossy, heart-shaped, long-stemmed; those at base form a rosette. Flowers are unscented, bluish violet, veined, up to 25mm across; spur (behind petals) is paler than petals, blunt-tipped, notched and curved. Fruits are triangular capsules that open to release the seeds.

KEY FACT
Common Dog-violets have their main flowering season in the spring, but they often flower again in the autumn. In fact, you can find them in flower in just about every month if you look hard enough.

STATUS AND COMMENTS
This is the most common violet in Britain and is encountered in very many habitats, including heaths, moors, pastures and rocky places.

SPOTTER'S CHART

LOCATION	DATE/TIME

EARLY DOG-VIOLET
Viola reichenbachiana

SIZE **Height to 12cm** HABITAT **Woodland, scrub, hedgerows, grassy banks** FLOWERING PERIOD **Mar–May**
HABIT **Low perennial**

KEY FACT Early Dog-violet is easily confused with Common Dog-violet, but the differences in habitat and distribution, along with subtle differences in leaf and flower shape, should help in its identification.

IDENTIFICATION

Leaves are heart-shaped (narrower than in Common Dog-violet). Flowers are unscented, pale violet; upper two petals are upright, close together and narrower than in Common Dog-violet; spur (behind petals) is darker than petals, pointed, unnotched and straight. Fruits are triangular capsules that open to release the seeds.

STATUS AND COMMENTS

This is a common violet in Britain, but less so in the N and W, and rare in Scotland. In woodlands with dry, chalky soils it is sometimes more common than Common Dog-violet.

SPOTTER'S CHART

LOCATION	DATE/TIME

WHITE BRYONY
Bryonia dioica

FACT FILE

SIZE **Height to 4m** HABITAT **Woodland, scrub, hedgerows** FLOWERING PERIOD **May–Aug** HABIT **Tall, spindly, climbing plant that twines up other plants; perennial**

KEY FACT Black Bryony can be confused with White Bryony, but has heart-shaped leaves and no tendrils. Every part of White Bryony is poisonous, including the berries.

IDENTIFICATION
Leaves are palmately lobed but variable, up to 7cm across, dull green. Flowers are greenish yellow, small, in groups on a short stem; male and female flowers are produced on different plants. Fruits are bright red berries in clusters. The plant climbs by means of tightly coiled, spiralling tendrils.

SPOTTER'S CHART

LOCATION	DATE/TIME

STATUS AND COMMENTS
White Bryony is common in **S, central and E England**, usually on calcareous soils, but is rare or absent in the rest of Britain. It is the only British member of the gourd family.

ENCHANTER'S-NIGHTSHADE
Circaea lutetiana

FACT FILE

SIZE **Height to 70cm** HABITAT **Woodland, scrub, hedgerows, banks; prefers shade** FLOWERING PERIOD **Jun–Aug** HABIT **Upright perennial**

IDENTIFICATION

Leaves are oval with a pointed tip and rounded base, up to 10cm long; in pairs, each pair at right angles to the one below. Flowers are very small, white, with two notched petals; in a loose spike at top of stem. Fruits are club-shaped with hooked bristles.

STATUS AND COMMENTS

Common in shady woods and scrub throughout much of Britain, but uncommon or rare in **N Scotland**.

KEY FACT

With one of the most romantic names among British wild flowers, this elegant little plant deserves to be better known. It was indeed used in magic, to protect against spells.

SPOTTER'S CHART

LOCATION	DATE/TIME

ROSEBAY WILLOWHERB
Chamerion angustifolium

SIZE Height to 1.5m **HABITAT** Woodland, scrub, wasteland, railway embankments **FLOWERING PERIOD** Jun–Sep **HABIT** Tall, upright perennial

IDENTIFICATION
Leaves are lanceolate, spirally arranged on stem, largest ones at base. Flowers are rose-purple, prominent, up to 3cm across; in spikes, opening gradually from bottom of spike to top. Fruits are pods that open to release clouds of downy seeds.

KEY FACT

Rosebay Willowherb spreads by means of both seeds and suckers. It was once popular in gardens, but its colonising habits make it unpopular with many gardeners today.

STATUS AND COMMENTS
Common in Britain in a wide variety of places. It swiftly colonises newly cleared areas, including burned sites, and for this reason is also known as Fireweed.

SPOTTER'S CHART

LOCATION	DATE/TIME

HOARY WILLOWHERB
Epilobium parviflorum

SIZE **Height to 75cm** HABITAT **Scrub, wasteland, marshy areas, stream-sides** FLOWERING PERIOD **Jun–Sep** HABIT **Upright perennial**

IDENTIFICATION
Leaves are oval, hairy. Flowers are pink, up to 10mm across, with notched petals. Fruits are pods containing cottony seeds. Stem is round and hairy. In many ways it is a smaller version of Great Willowherb, a key difference being that the leaves do not clasp the stem.

KEY FACT This plant is in many ways similar to its larger relative Great Willowherb, but that species is more restricted to damp places such as riversides and fens, and its leaves clasp the stem.

STATUS AND COMMENTS
Very common throughout Britain, except N Scotland. It has several close relatives, including Broad-leaved Willowherb, which is almost hairless and has rounder leaves.

SPOTTER'S CHART

LOCATION	DATE/TIME

SANICLE
Sanicula europaea

FACT FILE

SIZE Height to 60cm **HABITAT** Shady woodland, hedges and banks; prefers calcareous soils
FLOWERING PERIOD May–Aug **HABIT** Upright perennial

IDENTIFICATION
Leaves are palmate, rounded, deeply lobed, with up to five toothed lobes; dark, shiny green and superficially Parsley-like. Flowers are very small, pinkish; in dense, compact heads, usually with several heads on each flowering stem. Fruits are oval with hooked bristles.

STATUS AND COMMENTS
Found in woods throughout Britain, but is more common in deciduous woods, particularly those of Beech, in S Britain.

KEY FACT
A good place to look for the pretty but inconspicuous Sanicle is in a Beech wood, where it can form carpets in quite deep shade, often with few other plants around it.

SPOTTER'S CHART

LOCATION	DATE/TIME

SIZE Height to 1m **HABITAT** Woodland edges, hedgerows, shady banks, verges **FLOWERING PERIOD** Jun–Jul **HABIT** Upright biennial

IDENTIFICATION

Leaves are pinnate, divided two to three times, deep green, hairy. Flowers are white, in umbels up to 6cm across. Fruits are narrow, ridged, pointed. Stem is hairy, ridged, solid, with purple spots; swelling where leaves join stem. The plant looks very like the better-known Cow Parsley but is poisonous.

STATUS AND COMMENTS

Common throughout much of Britain, except N and W Scotland, where it is absent. This is one of the three most commonly encountered 'hedgerow' parsleys.

KEY FACT

Very similar to Cow Parsley and Upright Hedge-parsley, Rough Chervil can be identified by noting its flowering time: this is after Cow Parsley and before Upright Hedge-parsley. The purple spots on the stem of Rough Chervil are a further identifier.

SPOTTER'S CHART

LOCATION	DATE/TIME

COW PARSLEY
Anthriscus sylvestris

FACT FILE

SIZE Height to Im **HABITAT** Woodland edges, hedgerows, banks, verges, meadows. **FLOWERING PERIOD** Apr–Jun **HABIT** Upright perennial, billowing when in flower *en masse*

IDENTIFICATION
Leaves are pinnate, divided two to three times, bright green, slightly hairy, toothed; fern-like. Flowers are gleaming white, in umbels up to 6cm across, on delicate stalks. Fruits are smooth; they taper towards tip, where there is a small beak. Stem is hollow, unspotted (spotted in Rough Chervil).

KEY FACT Of the three common 'hedgerow' parsleys, this is the most common, and the earliest to flower. Unlike Rough Chervil, Cow Parsley is not poisonous, although it is inedible.

STATUS AND COMMENTS
Cow Parsley must surely be one of the most familiar of all British wild flowers, and can be found everywhere, except in parts of Scotland. It may be common, but when seen in profusion the impact and scent are memorable.

SPOTTER'S CHART

LOCATION	DATE/TIME

UPRIGHT HEDGE-PARSLEY
Torilis japonica

SIZE Height to 1m **HABITAT** Woodland edges, hedgerows, banks, verges **FLOWERING PERIOD** Jul–Aug **HABIT** Upright annual; very like the familiar Cow Parsley

IDENTIFICATION
Leaves are pinnate, divided two to three times, dull green, hairy, toothed; fern-like. Flowers are white or pinkish white, in umbels up to 3cm across. Fruits are egg-shaped, coated with hook-tipped bristles. Stem is solid, hairy, unspotted (spotted in Rough Chervil).

KEY FACT There are two other much less common hedge-parsleys: Spreading Hedge-parsley and Knotted Hedge-parsley. All spread by means of spiny fruits, which catch on fur and clothes.

STATUS AND COMMENTS
Widespread and locally common in S and central England, and in Wales, but absent from upland areas; a lowland species in N England and S and E Scotland.

SPOTTER'S CHART

LOCATION	DATE/TIME

ALEXANDERS
Smyrnium olusatrum

FACT FILE

SIZE Height to 1.25m HABITAT Woodland edges,
hedgerows, wasteland; often near the sea
FLOWERING PERIOD Apr–Jul HABIT Tall, upright biennial

IDENTIFICATION
Leaves are up to 30cm long, comprising three diamond-shaped, dark, shiny
green, toothed leaflets. Flowers are greenish yellow, in umbels up to 6cm
across. Fruits are oval, ridged, black. Stem is stout and solid. When seen in
clumps or colonies, the plant is
very striking and prominent.

STATUS AND COMMENTS
Locally common in S and E England,
and often seen near the sea. It
prefers calcareous soils. It was
once cultivated, the whole plant
being edible, and smells of celery.

KEY FACT
The only plant
found in Britain that might be
confused with Alexanders is
Fennel, but that species has
characteristic leaves that
are very feathery and an
unmistakable aniseed scent.

SPOTTER'S CHART

LOCATION	DATE/TIME

FACT FILE

SIZE Height to 20cm HABITAT Open woodland,
meadows, grassland FLOWERING PERIOD Apr–Jun
HABIT Delicate, slender, medium-sized perennial

IDENTIFICATION

Leaves are twice pinnate, with feathery, deeply divided leaflets, soon dying
back. Flowers are white, in umbels up to 5cm across. Fruits are oval and
slender, with projecting styles. Stem is smooth and hollow. The brown
root, or tuber, is edible, hence the plant's common name.

KEY FACT In May and
June, Pignut can be the most
common small umbellifer in
woodlands; the delicate feathery
leaves and petite overall
appearance help to identify it.

SPOTTER'S CHART

LOCATION	DATE/TIME

STATUS AND COMMENTS

Widespread and locally common
in suitable habitats throughout the
region; least numerous or locally
absent from parts of E and SE
England and NW Scotland.

HOGWEED
Heracleum sphondylium

FACT FILE

SIZE Height to 1.75m **HABITAT** Waste ground, field edges, roadsides, open woodland **FLOWERING PERIOD** May–Aug **HABIT** Upright biennial or perennial

IDENTIFICATION
Leaves are pinnate, up to 60cm long, deeply lobed and hairy. Flowers are creamy white, in large umbels up to 18cm across; scented. Fruits are flattened and smooth. Stem is hairy, ridged, hollow. The strong (some say unpleasant) scent of the flowers attracts many insects.

KEY FACT Hogweed has a huge – up to 5m – relative in the unmistakable Giant Hogweed. This plant should always be avoided as its sap causes extreme sensitivity to sunlight, leading to painful blisters.

STATUS AND COMMENTS
Widespread and generally common throughout most of the region, except on acid soils; least numerous or absent from parts of the Scottish Highlands and NW. It seeds prolifically.

SPOTTER'S CHART

LOCATION	DATE/TIME

FACT FILE SIZE Height to 1m HABITAT Roadsides, waste places, wood edges, hedgerows, banks, gardens FLOWERING PERIOD May–Aug HABIT Upright, spreading perennial

IDENTIFICATION
Leaves are broadly triangular in outline; trifoliate, the leaflets oval, pointed, toothed, mid-green. Flowers are white, in umbels up to 6cm across. Fruits are egg-shaped, ridged. Stem is hollow, ridged. The plant spreads by means of extensive mats of vigorous underground rhizomes.

KEY FACT This is one of the most pernicious and disliked garden weeds as it is very hard to eradicate – even the smallest piece of rhizome left in the ground after cultivation will grow into a new plant.

STATUS AND COMMENTS
Widespread and common throughout Britain. It was introduced from Europe, perhaps by the Romans, as an edible plant (the leaves can be boiled) and escaped from cultivation long ago.

SPOTTER'S CHART

LOCATION	DATE/TIME

WILD PARSNIP
Pastinaca sativa

SIZE Height to 1m **HABITAT** Grassland, meadows, waste places; almost always on dry, calcareous soils
FLOWERING PERIOD Jun–Sep **HABIT** Upright perennial

IDENTIFICATION
Leaves are pinnate; leaflets are broadly oval but deeply lobed and toothed, dark green. Flowers are yellow, in umbels up to 8cm across. Fruits are flattened, oval. Stem is hollow, furrowed. The plant has a pungent scent if rubbed, but the sap can cause severe blisters.

STATUS AND COMMENTS
Widespread and locally common only in central-S and S England; restricted to coastal limestone areas in SW and N England and S Wales; absent from Scotland.

KEY FACT
The Garden Parsnip is descended from this plant, and occasionally will also seed outside of cultivation. The similar Pepper-saxifrage also has yellow flowers but its leaves are fennel-like.

SPOTTER'S CHART

LOCATION	DATE/TIME

HEMLOCK WATER-DROPWORT
Oenanthe crocata

FACT FILE SIZE **Height to 1.5m** HABITAT **Stream-sides, pond edges, wet hedgerows, damp woodlands** FLOWERING PERIOD **Jun–Aug** HABIT **Tall, straight biennial**

IDENTIFICATION

Leaves are triangular in outline, pinnate, divided two to four times; leaflets are glossy, oval, deeply lobed, tapering to base; leaf stalks sheathe stem. Flowers are white, in umbels up to 10cm across, at top of plant; they have both bracts and bracteoles. Fruits are oblong with two horns (styles) at top. Stem is hollow, cylindrical, grooved. The plant smells of Parsley.

STATUS AND COMMENTS

Locally common in **S** and **W** Britain, where it is nearly always found close to water or in wet places. It is rare or absent from much of the rest of Britain.

KEY FACT

Hemlock Water-dropwort is one of Britain's most poisonous plants, every part being deadly. It often forms large clumps, and may grow in water as well as beside it.

SPOTTER'S CHART

LOCATION	DATE/TIME

WILD ANGELICA
Angelica sylvestris

SIZE Height to 2m **HABITAT** Open woodland,
stream-sides, meadows, pastures, cliffs **FLOWERING PERIOD** Jul–Sep
HABIT Tall, robust, almost hairless perennial

FACT FILE

IDENTIFICATION
Leaves are pinnate, divided two
to three times; leaflets are oval,
pointed, with serrated edges;
lower leaves are up to 60cm
long; upper leaves are very
small, emerging from sheaths
from which flowering stems
appear. Flowers are white or
pink, in umbels up to 15cm
across. Fruits are oval,
flattened. Stem is purple.

STATUS AND COMMENTS
Found throughout Britain,
nearly always in places where
the conditions are damp. It is
quite often found by the sea,
where it might be on top or
at the base of cliffs.

KEY FACT Garden
Angelica is larger than Wild
Angelica and has green, not
purple, stems. Hogweed might
be confused with them, but they
are almost hairless whereas
Hogweed is very hairy.

SPOTTER'S CHART

LOCATION	DATE/TIME

GREATER BURNET-SAXIFRAGE
Pimpinella major

FACT FILE SIZE Height to 1m HABITAT Woodland edges, banks, hedgerows; prefers shade FLOWERING PERIOD Jun–Sep HABIT Erect perennial

IDENTIFICATION
Leaves are pinnate; leaflets are up to 8cm long, oval, toothed, glossy and dark. Flowers are white, sometimes pink (colour tends to vary from region to region); in umbels up to 6cm across, these flat and at top of plant. Fruits are oval, ridged. Stem is smooth, ridged, hollow.

STATUS AND COMMENTS
Locally common in parts of Britain, with strongholds in central England. It is rare or absent from many other parts of the country. It prefers heavier soils and does best in shade.

KEY FACT

The closely related Burnet-saxifrage is much smaller and prefers very different habitats: dry, light, calcareous soils in open conditions.

SPOTTER'S CHART

LOCATION	DATE/TIME

PRIMROSE
Primula vulgaris

FACT FILE

SIZE **Height to 20cm** HABITAT **Woodland, woodland edges, banks, hedgerows, grassland** FLOWERING PERIOD **Feb–May** HABIT **Compact, cushiony perennial**

KEY FACT
Although Primroses flower at their peak in spring, they can usually be found in flower in ones or twos throughout the year if looked for carefully, especially in traditionally managed woodland.

IDENTIFICATION
Leaves are oval, up to 12cm long, wrinkled, dark green; they grow from a basal rosette. Flowers are yellow with bright yellow centres, occasionally pink when crossed with cultivated forms; borne singly on long, slender, hairy stems rising from leaf rosette; sweetly scented in sunshine. Fruits are small capsules.

STATUS AND COMMENTS
Widespread and common throughout Britain. They can grow in very large numbers if the conditions suit them and if they receive the right amount of light.

SPOTTER'S CHART

LOCATION	DATE/TIME

FACT FILE

SIZE Height to 25cm HABITAT Meadows, pastures, woodland rides and edges, banks, hedgerows FLOWERING PERIOD Apr–May HABIT Upright perennial

IDENTIFICATION
Leaves are oval, up to 15cm long, wrinkled, hairy, dark green; they grow from a basal rosette. Flowers are orange-yellow, occasionally orange or purple-brown when crossed with cultivated forms; in heads of up to 20 on long stems that rise from leaf rosette; sweetly scented in sunshine. Fruits are small capsules.

STATUS AND COMMENTS
Widespread in England and Wales, but less common in Scotland. Although they are thought of as flowers of dry, chalky places, they can also be found in damp places and in semi-shade.

KEY FACT

Cowslips are much less common than they were half a century ago due to habitat loss, but when given the opportunity they will grow prolifically from seed in a wide variety of soils and conditions.

SPOTTER'S CHART

LOCATION	DATE/TIME

OXLIP
Primula elatior

SIZE **Height to 20cm** HABITAT **Open woodland, most often traditionally managed** FLOWERING PERIOD **Mar–May** HABIT **Upright perennial**

IDENTIFICATION

Leaves are oval, long, rather crinkled, downy, pale green; they grow from a basal rosette. Flowers are pale yellow, rather like those of Primrose; on long stems that rise from leaf rosette in heads of up to 20, drooping and all facing the same way. Fruits are small capsules.

KEY FACT Oxlip can be confused with False Oxlip, a naturally occurring hybrid of Cowslip and Primrose. However, False Oxlip flowers do not all fall in the same direction, unlike those of true Oxlip.

STATUS AND COMMENTS

Oxlips have a particular and restricted distribution: they are nearly all found in woodlands on clay soils in central and E England, with strongholds in Suffolk, Essex and Buckinghamshire.

SPOTTER'S CHART

LOCATION	DATE/TIME

CREEPING-JENNY
Lysimachia nummularia

FACT FILE

SIZE **Height to 6cm** HABITAT **Open woodland, banks, meadows** FLOWERING PERIOD **Jun–Aug** HABIT **Creeping, spreading, rooting perennial**

IDENTIFICATION
Leaves are heart-shaped to round, up to 3cm long, in opposite pairs on stem. Flowers are yellow, up to 25mm across, bell-shaped (as if half-open), on stalks that are shorter than leaves. Fruits are small capsules. Stems are creeping, and are very vigorous in favourable conditions.

KEY FACT
The natural distribution of Creeping-Jenny in Britain is complicated by the fact that it is a popular garden plant, grown as ground cover and to brighten paths and paved areas.

STATUS AND COMMENTS
Quite common in S and E England, but is less common or rare in the W and N. It prefers damp conditions.

SPOTTER'S CHART

LOCATION	DATE/TIME

YELLOW PIMPERNEL
Lysimachia nemorum

FACT FILE

SIZE Height to 10cm **HABITAT** Open woodland,
shady hedge banks, meadows **FLOWERING PERIOD** May–Aug
HABIT Creeping, spreading perennial

KEY FACT

Yellow Pimpernel is
closely related to Yellow Loosestrife,
a tall, upright and robust plant, with
dark green lanceolate leaves.

IDENTIFICATION
Leaves are oval, pointed at tip, up to
4cm long, in opposite pairs on stem.
Flowers are yellow, up to 12mm across,
star-shaped, on stalks that are longer
than leaves. Fruits are small capsules.

STATUS AND COMMENTS
Common throughout much of Britain.
It is related to Creeping-Jenny; both are
found in similar, often damp, habitats,
but Creeping-Jenny has a much more
restricted natural distribution.

SPOTTER'S CHART

LOCATION	DATE/TIME

HEDGE BINDWEED
Calystegia sepium

SIZE **Height to 3m** HABITAT **Woodland edges, hedgerows, embankments, waste ground** FLOWERING PERIOD **Jun–Sep** HABIT **Tall, climbing, twining perennial**

IDENTIFICATION

Leaves are oblong to arrow-shaped, up to 12cm long. Flowers are white (sometimes pink), trumpet-shaped, up to 4cm across, borne singly on long stems. Fruits are small capsules. The tough, twining stems grow anticlockwise up trees, shrubs, posts and fences.

STATUS AND COMMENTS

The large, handsome flowers of Hedge Bindweed brighten hedgerows and banks throughout S Britain, but the plant is more scarce in the N.

KEY FACT

Large Bindweed can grow even taller than Hedge Bindweed. The key difference between the two is the green bracts at the base of the flowers: in Large Bindweed they overlap and in Hedge Bindweed they do not.

SPOTTER'S CHART

LOCATION	DATE/TIME

FIELD BINDWEED
Convolvulus arvensis

FACT FILE

SIZE **Climbing or trailing** HABITAT **Fields, hedgerows, embankments, waste ground, gardens** FLOWERING PERIOD **Jun–Sep** HABIT **Creeping perennial**

IDENTIFICATION
Leaves are oblong to arrow-shaped, up to 4cm long, borne alternately up stems. Flowers are white, or pink with broad white stripes; funnel-shaped, up to 28mm across, growing singly on long stems. Fruits are small globular capsules containing four seeds. The twining stems grow anticlockwise.

KEY FACT
This is one of the most loathed garden weeds. Its deep, widespread roots are almost impossible to remove without breaking, and from each bit of root left behind grows a new plant.

SPOTTER'S CHART

LOCATION	DATE/TIME

STATUS AND COMMENTS
Widespread and generally common in central and S England; mostly absent from upland areas in Wales and N England; in Scotland, mainly in the S.

BILBERRY
Vaccinium myrtillus

FACT FILE

SIZE Height to 70cm **HABITAT** Woodlands, heaths, moors, banks; on acid soils **FLOWERING PERIOD** Apr–Jul
HABIT Deciduous shrub

IDENTIFICATION
Leaves are oval, finely toothed, up to 3cm long; bright green. Flowers are pink, globe-shaped, drooping, up to 6mm long. Fruits are black berries; edible. Stems are woody.

STATUS AND COMMENTS
Bilberry can be found, in the right dry places on acid soils, throughout Britain, but is not so common in E England.

KEY FACT
Sometimes Bilberry becomes the dominant plant in such places as dry moors or in open oak woods in Wales and the W. The berries can be eaten raw or in preserves.

SPOTTER'S CHART

LOCATION	DATE/TIME

YELLOW BIRD'S-NEST
Monotropa hypopitys

SIZE **Height to 10cm** HABITAT **Woodlands, primarily of Beech or conifers; also dune slacks** FLOWERING PERIOD **Jun–Sep** HABIT **Upright with a bending top**

KEY FACT Even though it looks so peculiar and unusual, Yellow Bird's-nest may be confused with one other plant in Britain: Bird's-nest Orchid. However, that species is taller, brown (not yellow), and has distinct two-lobed lips to the brown flowers.

IDENTIFICATION
Leaves do not resemble leaves in the accepted sense: they are scale-like, yellow, clasping stem. Flowers are yellow, up to 15mm long, bell-shaped, in drooping spikes. Fruits are small, globular capsules. Stem is yellow – the plant contains no chlorophyll at all.

STATUS AND COMMENTS
This plant has very specialised habitat requirements, usually growing in the dark depths of a Beech or conifer wood. It is found occasionally in England, and much more rarely elsewhere.

SPOTTER'S CHART

LOCATION	DATE/TIME

LESSER PERIWINKLE
Vinca minor

FACT FILE

SIZE **Height to 75cm** HABITAT **Woods, hedgerows, scrub, gardens** FLOWERING PERIOD **Feb–May**
HABIT **Trailing evergreen perennial**

IDENTIFICATION

Leaves are oval with a pointed tip, borne in pairs; dark, shiny green.
Flowers are deep blue, up to 30mm across, with five petals. The long,
creeping stems root at
intervals; upright flowering
stems grow at these points.

STATUS AND COMMENTS

Possibly native to **S England**, Lesser Periwinkle
has a scattered distribution
throughout Britain, often
as a garden escape.

KEY FACT

Lesser Periwinkle can
cover huge areas if left to grow
unchecked. Its close relative, Greater
Periwinkle, is just as vigorous, but has
significantly bigger flowers and broader
leaves, and roots only at the end of the
creeping stems.

SPOTTER'S CHART

LOCATION	DATE/TIME

WOODRUFF
Galium odoratum

FACT FILE

SIZE **Height to 25cm** HABITAT **Shady woodlands, gardens; prefers calcareous soils** FLOWERING PERIOD **May–Jun** HABIT **Petite, elegant, carpet-forming perennial**

IDENTIFICATION
Leaves are lanceolate, shiny green, with tiny forward-pointing prickles on edge; in whorls of six to eight, these quite widely separated along stem. Flowers are white, star-shaped, up to 4mm across; in small clusters on long stem. Fruits are round, tiny, with hooked spines. Stem is square and hairless.

KEY FACT

Woodruff (sometimes called Sweet Woodruff) is sweetly scented, like hay (especially if rubbed or when dried). Its pretty appearance and habit of forming carpets in shady places make it a popular garden plant, though it can spread too quickly for tidy gardeners.

STATUS AND COMMENTS
A woodland plant, locally common in much of Britain, but occasional in East Anglia and uncommon in N Scotland.

SPOTTER'S CHART

LOCATION	DATE/TIME

COMMON CLEAVERS
Galium aparine

FACT FILE

SIZE Height to 1.3m HABITAT Hedgerows, wood edges and rides, wasteland FLOWERING PERIOD May–Sep HABIT Scrambling annual

IDENTIFICATION

Leaves are linear-lanceolate, shiny green, with tiny backward-pointing prickles on edge; in whorls of six to eight, these quite widely separated along stem. Flowers are white, tiny; in small clusters in leaf axils. Fruits are round, tiny, with hooked spines. Stem is square with downward-pointing prickles on edges.

KEY FACT Goosegrass is one of this species' other common names (geese and hens like to eat it), as is Sticky Willy, which is a good description of its clinging properties ('cleave' also means to stick or cling).

STATUS AND COMMENTS

Common throughout Britain and found in a remarkable variety of habitats, from woodlands to coasts and from wild places to arable fields.

SPOTTER'S CHART

LOCATION	DATE/TIME

WILD MADDER
Rubia peregrina

FACT FILE

SIZE Height to 2m **HABITAT** Scrub, woodlands, headlands, cliffs; most often near the sea **FLOWERING PERIOD** Jun–Aug **HABIT** Sprawling, clambering, evergreen perennial

KEY FACT
Distribution and habitat should help to identify this plant; it also looks very distinct, with leathery evergreen leaves and an overall prickliness.

IDENTIFICATION
Leaves are lanceolate, dark green, leathery, with distinct curved prickles on edge; in whorls of four to six, these quite widely separated along stem. Flowers are greenish white, up to 6mm across; on long stem growing from leaf axils. Fruits are round, black. Stem is four-angled with downward-pointing prickles on edges.

STATUS AND COMMENTS
Wild Madder has a very restricted distribution in Britain, being found primarily on the coasts of S and SW England, Wales, the Isles of Scilly and the Channel Isles.

SPOTTER'S CHART

LOCATION	DATE/TIME

WOOD FORGET-ME-NOT
Myosotis sylvatica

FACT FILE

SIZE **Height to 50cm** HABITAT **Woodlands;**
occasionally meadows and mountains FLOWERING PERIOD **Apr–Jul**
HABIT **Upright, many-branched perennial**

IDENTIFICATION
Leaves are oblong, hairy. Flowers are sky blue, up to 10mm across, with five petals; in curved clusters. Fruits are dark brown; on comparatively long, spreading stalks. Stem is hairy.

KEY FACT There are 10 or so species of forget-me-not that are found in Britain, many of them very similar. Wood Forget-me-not has larger flowers than most and is much the tallest.

STATUS AND COMMENTS
As its name suggests, this forget-me-not is most likely found in woods, though it also occurs in other habitats; it prefers damp situations. It is locally common in **S Britain**.

SPOTTER'S CHART

LOCATION	DATE/TIME

CHANGING FORGET-ME-NOT
Myosotis discolor

FACT FILE

SIZE **Height to 20cm** HABITAT **Field edges,
hedgerows, waste places, grasslands; dry, bare, sandy places**
FLOWERING PERIOD **Apr–Sep** HABIT **Branched annual**

KEY FACT
Similar common relatives include Early Forget-me-not, which is very small with blue flowers, and the bigger Field Forget-me-not, which is the most widespread of the group.

IDENTIFICATION
Leaves are oblong, downy. Flowers are pale yellow or creamy at first, turning blue; up to 3mm across. Fruits are dark brown, carried on comparatively short stalks. Stem is hairy.

STATUS AND COMMENTS
Common throughout Britain in the dry, often disturbed, sandy soils that it prefers.

SPOTTER'S CHART

LOCATION	DATE/TIME

SIZE **Height to 20cm** HABITAT **Woodlands, hedgerows, damp grassland** FLOWERING PERIOD **Apr–Jul** HABIT **Spreading, creeping perennial**

IDENTIFICATION

Leaves are oval; dark, shiny green (sometimes bronzy); lower leaves, up to 7cm long, form a basal rosette; upper ones are widely spread up stem in opposite pairs. Flowers are vivid purple-blue, up to 15mm long, with a prominent, veined lower lip; upper lip is not visible. Fruits are nutlets. Stem is hairy on two opposite sides.

KEY FACT

Bugle (its common name may originally have been Abuga and nothing to do with musical instruments) often forms thick mats, where its prominent flower stems stand out attractively. The striking, unusually shaped flowers are also sometimes pink or white.

STATUS AND COMMENTS

Common and widespread through much of Britain, especially in the S.

SPOTTER'S CHART

LOCATION	DATE/TIME

SELFHEAL
Prunella vulgaris

FACT FILE

SIZE Height to 20cm HABITAT Grassland, banks,
woodland rides, waste ground FLOWERING PERIOD Jun–Sep
HABIT Spreading, creeping perennial

IDENTIFICATION
Leaves are oval, pointed at tip, widest at base, bright green; lower leaves
are stalked, upper ones unstalked; in opposite pairs up stem. Flowers are
violet, up to 15mm long; in a dense, oblong terminal spike that appears
purple thanks to purplish bracts and calyx teeth. Fruits are nutlets.

KEY FACT
Selfheal can
be confused with Bugle, but its
flowers have a prominent upper
lip (this is not apparent in Bugle),
and Bugle has bluer flowers and
shinier, blunt-tipped leaves.

STATUS AND COMMENTS
Common throughout Britain,
and often seen as a lawn weed.
It takes it name from the fact that
it was once considered a medicine
that could be used to treat many
ailments without the help of a
medical professional.

SPOTTER'S CHART

LOCATION	DATE/TIME

FACT FILE

SIZE **Height to 60cm** HABITAT **Woodlands, rough grassland, heaths, dunes; prefers dry, acid soils** FLOWERING PERIOD **Jun–Sep** HABIT **Upright, downy perennial**

IDENTIFICATION

Leaves are oval, heart-shaped at base, wrinkled, toothed; in opposite pairs on stem. Flowers are yellowish green, up to 6mm long, with a wide lower lip and no apparent upper lip, leaving red stamens exposed; in opposite pairs on a leafless spike. Fruits comprise four nutlets. Stem is square and hairy.

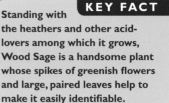

KEY FACT

Standing with the heathers and other acid-lovers among which it grows, Wood Sage is a handsome plant whose spikes of greenish flowers and large, paired leaves help to make it easily identifiable.

STATUS AND COMMENTS

Common in its preferred habitats throughout much of Britain, but uncommon to rare in East Anglia. Its smell is reminiscent of Hops, and like that plant it was once used in brewing.

SPOTTER'S CHART

LOCATION	DATE/TIME

GROUND IVY
Glechoma hederacea

FACT FILE

SIZE Height to 25cm **HABITAT** Woodlands, hedgerows, grassland, waste places **FLOWERING PERIOD** Mar–May
HABIT Creeping, rooting perennial

IDENTIFICATION
Leaves are round to kidney-shaped, blunt-toothed, long-stemmed. Flowers are mauve, up to 20mm long, with a spotted, three-lobed lower lip; in whorls of up to four arising from leaf axils. Fruits are nutlets. The creeping stems root at regular intervals.

STATUS AND COMMENTS
Common throughout Britain, except in N Scotland, where it is rare. The plant has a pungent aroma if crushed and was once used to flavour beers.

> **KEY FACT**
> Ground Ivy takes its name not from the shape of its leaves (which are not Ivy-shaped) but because, like Ivy, it creeps and roots as it goes, and because it can remain green throughout the winter.

SPOTTER'S CHART

LOCATION	DATE/TIME

FACT FILE

SIZE **Height to 60cm** HABITAT **Woodland edges, hedgerows, verges, waste places** FLOWERING PERIOD **Mar–Nov** HABIT **Upright, clump-forming perennial**

IDENTIFICATION

Leaves are heart-shaped, pointed, toothed, up to 7cm long. Flowers are bright white, up to 30mm long, with a hooded upper lip and three-lobed lower lip; in whorls along top half of stem. Fruits are nutlets. Stem is square. The plant spreads and forms clumps by means of creeping rhizomes.

KEY FACT

The leaves of White Dead-nettle look very like those of Common Nettle, but they do not sting. As soon as the striking white flowers appear, all possible confusion between the two is gone.

STATUS AND COMMENTS

Found throughout Britain, White Dead-nettle is most common in the S, becoming less common in the N and uncommon in N Scotland.

SPOTTER'S CHART

LOCATION	DATE/TIME

RED DEAD-NETTLE
Lamium purpureum

SIZE Height to 30cm **HABITAT** Waste places, verges and hedgerows **FLOWERING PERIOD** Mar–Oct **HABIT** Short and spreading, or upright, annual

KEY FACT In the spring, and when not in flower, Red Dead-nettle can resemble its close relative White Dead-nettle. However, Red Dead-nettle is frequently reddish all over, not just the flowers, and is usually a much smaller plant.

IDENTIFICATION
Leaves are heart-shaped, blunt-toothed, up to 7cm long, often purplish; in opposite pairs on stem. Flowers are pinkish purple, up to 18mm long, with a hooded upper lip and three-lobed lower lip; in whorls along top half of stem. Fruits are nutlets. Stem is four-angled, hairy, often reddish. The plant frequently branches from the base to form a clump.

STATUS AND COMMENTS
Common throughout Britain, except in N Scotland, and a familiar weed of vegetable patches and allotments. It has a pungent aroma when crushed.

SPOTTER'S CHART

LOCATION	DATE/TIME

FACT FILE SIZE Height to 60cm HABITAT Waste places, bare ground, verges, shingle FLOWERING PERIOD Jul–Sep HABIT Very variable in height, from tall to stunted; annual

IDENTIFICATION
Leaves are up to 8cm long, lanceolate, narrow and narrowing further to base, with a pointed tip and slightly toothed. Flowers are reddish

KEY FACT
Common Hemp-nettle is a common, closely related plant, found in similar habitats. However, it is often taller, and has paler pink flowers, wider leaves and prominent swollen leaf joints.

purple with white spots on lip, up to 25mm long; in whorls near top of stem. Fruits are nutlets. The hairy stem is not swollen at the leaf joints.

STATUS AND COMMENTS
Red Hemp-nettle has a restricted distribution in Britain. It is most likely to be seen in S England, on calcareous soils, but is rare in Wales and very rare in Scotland. It can be a very short, stunted plant in some locations.

SPOTTER'S CHART

LOCATION	DATE/TIME

YELLOW ARCHANGEL
Lamiastrum galeobdolon

SIZE **Height to 60cm** HABITAT **Woodlands, hedgerows; prefers richer or calcareous soils** FLOWERING PERIOD **Apr–Jun** HABIT **Upright perennial**

IDENTIFICATION
Leaves are up to 7cm long, oval, pointed at tip, toothed; in opposite pairs up stem. Flowers are bright yellow with thin red lines; in whorls up stem arising from leaf joints. Fruits are nutlets. The plant grows long, leafy runners that help it to spread and form carpets.

KEY FACT A variegated, cultivated subspecies of Yellow Archangel, ssp. *argentatum*, frequently escapes from cultivation, invading woods and competing with its wild relative.

STATUS AND COMMENTS
One of the quintessential, beautiful wild flowers of English woodlands, especially in recently cut, traditionally managed woodland. It is common in England and Wales, but uncommon to rare in Scotland.

SPOTTER'S CHART

LOCATION	DATE/TIME

HEDGE WOUNDWORT
Stachys sylvatica

FACT FILE
SIZE **Height to 1m** HABITAT **Woodlands, hedgerows, waste ground, verges** FLOWERING PERIOD **Jun–Sep**
HABIT **Tall, upright, unbranched perennial**

KEY FACT

Betony is a close relative. It has a basal rosette of corrugated, blunt-ended, oblong leaves, and a distinctive compact, very pretty spike of wine-red flowers.

IDENTIFICATION

Leaves are up to 9cm long, oval/heart-shaped with a pointed tip, toothed; bottom leaves are much larger. Flowers are reddish purple with white blotches on lip; up to 18mm long, in loose whorls near top of plant. Fruits are nutlets. The plant has a very pungent odour if rubbed.

STATUS AND COMMENTS

Common throughout Britain, Hedge Woundwort may be so widespread because it was once highly valued as a medicinal plant. One of its uses was as a dressing to stop bleeding.

SPOTTER'S CHART

LOCATION	DATE/TIME

COMMON CALAMINT
Calamintha ascendens

FACT FILE

SIZE **Height to 50cm** HABITAT **Hedgerows, woodland edges, banks, scrub** FLOWERING PERIOD **Jul–Sep**
HABIT **Medium-sized, upright perennial**

KEY FACT

The much more common Wild Basil is very similar in many ways, but has darker flowers in denser whorls, and prefers more open habitats.

IDENTIFICATION
Leaves are up to 4cm long, oval, slightly toothed, dark green. Flowers are pale pink with darker blotches on lower lip; up to 10mm long, in whorls scattered up stem. Fruits are nutlets. The plant smells strongly of mint when rubbed.

STATUS AND COMMENTS
Common Calamint is not actually common at all, being restricted to chalk and limestone, mainly in S England. It is rare or very local in Wales and N England, and absent from Scotland.

SPOTTER'S CHART

LOCATION	DATE/TIME

BASTARD BALM
Melittis melissophyllum

SIZE **Height to 50cm** HABITAT **Hedgerows, open woodland, banks** FLOWERING PERIOD **May–Jul** HABIT **Upright, often multi-stemmed perennial**

IDENTIFICATION

Leaves are up to 8cm long, oval, toothed, bright green. Flowers are off-white, tinged with pink or purple; up to 40mm long, in whorls scattered up stem; prominent and scented. Fruits are nutlets. Stem is hairy. The plant has a pungent scent when rubbed.

STATUS AND COMMENTS

An uncommon, strikingly handsome plant, found primarily in S and SW England, as well as in Wales. It does not grow on calcareous soils.

KEY FACT

The unusual common name possibly arose to distinguish this plant from the similar garden herb Lemon Balm, which smells strongly of lemons.

SPOTTER'S CHART

LOCATION	DATE/TIME

IVY BROOMRAPE
Orobanche hederae

SIZE Height to 50cm **HABITAT** Woodland, hedgerows; usually on calcareous soils **FLOWERING PERIOD** May–Jul **HABIT** Upright; parasitic, and with no green parts

IDENTIFICATION
Leaves are scale-like, brown, held against stem. Flowers are creamy white, streaked with pink or purple; up to 20mm long, in spikes. Fruits are capsules containing tiny seeds. Stem is purple-brown, occasionally yellow. The plant has no chlorophyll and no green parts.

KEY FACT
You are unlikely to mistake a broomrape for any other plant (except perhaps Toothwort). Common Broomrape is very similar to Ivy Broomrape, but is stouter and often has pinker flowers.

STATUS AND COMMENTS
Ivy Broomrape is entirely dependent on Ivy, from which it gains all of its nourishment. It is a locally common plant, mainly restricted in its distribution to the S and W.

SPOTTER'S CHART

LOCATION	DATE/TIME

FACT FILE

SIZE Height to 25cm HABITAT Woodland, hedgerows; usually on rich soils FLOWERING PERIOD Apr–May HABIT Short, stout, creeping perennial

IDENTIFICATION

Leaves are scale-like, creamy white, held against stem. Flowers are tinged pink, up to 18mm long; on drooping, one-sided spikes. Fruits are capsules containing tiny seeds. Stem is creamy white. The plant has no chlorophyll and no green parts.

KEY FACT You might confuse Toothwort with a broomrape, but the broomrapes are taller, and they lack the overall creamy-white appearance and one-sided flower spike.

STATUS AND COMMENTS

Toothwort is parasitic on Hazel and other plants, from which it gains all its nourishment. It is widespread, though only locally common, found throughout Britain except N Scotland.

SPOTTER'S CHART

LOCATION	DATE/TIME

PURPLE TOOTHWORT
Lathraea clandestina

FACT FILE

SIZE Flower spike to 10cm; rest of plant barely visible
HABITAT Damp woodland **FLOWERING PERIOD** Mar–May
HABIT Only flower spike is visible; perennial

KEY FACT

Purple Toothwort is very different in appearance from its relatives the broomrapes and Toothwort, but might be confused with Lousewort. That species is similar in habit and flower appearance, but has a visible stem and prefers open habitats on acid soils.

IDENTIFICATION
Leaves are scale-like, purplish, hardly visible. Flowers are purple, up to 5cm long, tube-like; in a tight group seemingly growing straight out of the ground. Fruits are capsules. The plant is parasitic, and has no chlorophyll and no green parts.

STATUS AND COMMENTS
Purple Toothwort is parasitic on such damp-loving trees as willows and alders. It is an introduced plant, with a very localised distribution.

SPOTTER'S CHART

LOCATION	DATE/TIME

FACT FILE

SIZE Height to 2m HABITAT Woods, hedges, waste places, beaches FLOWERING PERIOD Jun–Sep HABIT Scrambling, clambering perennial

IDENTIFICATION

Leaves are oval, pointed at tip, on longish stalks; often with two conspicuous leaflets at base. Flowers are purple, up to 15mm across, with bright yellow projecting anthers. Fruits are small and egg-shaped, starting off green and ripening through yellow to red; they are poisonous.

KEY FACT

Many people will know this plant by its other common name, Woody Nightshade. The 'Woody' part of this name describes the lower part of the stem, while the 'Nightshade' part is a reminder of its (frequently very poisonous) family.

SPOTTER'S CHART

LOCATION	DATE/TIME

STATUS AND COMMENTS

Common and widespread throughout Britain, except in the far N of Scotland. Its colourful flowers and fruits make it conspicuous and well known.

GREAT MULLEIN
Verbascum thapsus

SIZE Height to 2m HABITAT Waste or disturbed ground, hedges, verges, banks FLOWERING PERIOD Jun–Aug HABIT Upright biennial

Six or so mulleins are encountered in Britain. Of these, Great Mullein is the most widespread and one of the tallest; only Hoary Mullein is as big, but it is restricted to East Anglia.

IDENTIFICATION
Leaves are oval, woolly, grey-green, on winged stems; much larger at base, where they form a rosette in first year. Flowers are bright yellow, up to 35mm across; very dense, on tall spikes; each plant might have several flowering spikes. Fruits are capsules. The whole plant looks and feels woolly.

STATUS AND COMMENTS
This is a common plant throughout Britain. It is still often known by its country name of Aaron's Rod.

SPOTTER'S CHART

LOCATION	DATE/TIME

FACT FILE

SIZE **Height to 1m** HABITAT **Waste or disturbed ground, hedges, banks, open woodland** FLOWERING PERIOD **Jun–Aug** HABIT **Upright biennial or short-lived perennial**

KEY FACT Dark Mullein is smaller than other British mulleins. Moth Mullein also has purple hairs on its stamens, but it has larger, single flowers on longish stalks.

IDENTIFICATION
Leaves are oval; lower leaves are larger, on long stalks, darker above, paler beneath; upper leaves are much smaller and unstalked. Flowers are bright yellow, up to 2cm across, with very conspicuous purple hairs on stamens; flowering spikes form a mass of yellow blooms. Fruits are capsules.

STATUS AND COMMENTS
Locally common in S Britain and uncommon further N. It prefers dry, sandy or calcareous soils.

SPOTTER'S CHART

LOCATION	DATE/TIME

COMMON FIGWORT
Scrophularia nodosa

FACT FILE

SIZE **Height to 90cm** HABITAT **Woods, shady hedgerows** FLOWERING PERIOD **Jun–Sep** HABIT **Upright, narrow biennial**

IDENTIFICATION
Leaves are oval, pointed at tip, sharply toothed. Flowers are small (up to 1cm long) and unusual; rich red-brown with two lips, the upper one protruding and looking rather like two tiny mouse ears. Fruits are oval capsules. Stem is square.

KEY FACT The strangely attractive flowers often go unnoticed since the entire plant is self-effacing, despite being quite large. Wasps certainly notice it, however, as they are attracted by the scent of the flowers.

STATUS AND COMMENTS
Locally common throughout Britain, except in N Scotland. It is easy to miss, and often grows in less damp conditions than some books suggest.

SPOTTER'S CHART

LOCATION	DATE/TIME

GERMANDER SPEEDWELL
Veronica chamaedrys

FACT FILE

SIZE Height to 20cm HABITAT Woods, hedgerows, grassy banks FLOWERING PERIOD Mar–Jul
HABIT Short, creeping, upright perennial

IDENTIFICATION

Leaves are oval, up to 2cm long, prominently toothed, hairy; sometimes with a short stalk, sometimes unstalked. Flowers are bright blue with a white centre, up to 12mm across; in clusters at top of upright flower spike. Fruits are heart-shaped, hairy capsules. Flowering stem has a line of hairs on each side.

KEY FACT Wood Speedwell is very similar, but its flowering stem is hairy all round, its leaves have longer stalks, and its flowers are smaller. There are other similar speedwells, but these grow in different habitats.

STATUS AND COMMENTS

Common throughout Britain. Its creeping stems root at intervals to create new plants.

SPOTTER'S CHART

LOCATION	DATE/TIME

FOXGLOVE
Digitalis purpurea

FACT FILE

SIZE Height to 1.8m HABITAT Woodland glades, hedgerows, banks, cliffs FLOWERING PERIOD Jun–Aug HABIT Tall, upright, imposing perennial or biennial

KEY FACT

Bumblebees are frequent visitors to Foxglove flowers, often emerging with their furry bodies covered in pollen. Highly poisonous, Foxgloves are the source of the cardiac drug digitalis.

IDENTIFICATION
Leaves are oval to lanceolate, up to 30cm long, wrinkled; leaf stalks are winged; lower leaves are large and form a rosette in first year. Flowers are light purple (sometimes white or pink), tube-shaped, with prominent dots on lower lip; held on one side of upright flowering spike. Fruits are capsules.

STATUS AND COMMENTS
Common throughout Britain in a wide variety of habitats, from open moorland to sea cliffs and from woodlands to gardens.

SPOTTER'S CHART

LOCATION	DATE/TIME

FACT FILE

SIZE **Height to 45cm** HABITAT **Open woodlands, banks, heaths** FLOWERING PERIOD **May–Oct** HABIT **Thin, branched, semi-parasitic annual**

IDENTIFICATION

Leaves are oval to lanceolate, narrow, up to 8cm long. Flowers are yellow, up to 15mm long, tube-shaped, with two lips; in pairs in leaf axils. Fruits are oval with a pointed tip. Stem and overall appearance are variable: the plant is sometimes tall and upright, sometimes bushy, but usually branched.

KEY FACT

Common Cow-wheat bears no resemblance to wheat plants, but the seeds were once commonly used to make bread, and cows were said to like the stems and leaves.

STATUS AND COMMENTS

Found throughout Britain, most often in woodlands with airy canopies or in cleared areas, this plant is unassuming and easily missed even when in flower. It continues to flower until well into the autumn.

SPOTTER'S CHART

LOCATION	DATE/TIME

MOSCHATEL
Adoxa moschatellina

FACT FILE

SIZE **Height to 10cm** HABITAT **Woodlands, shady hedgerows, rocky mountainsides** FLOWERING PERIOD **Apr–May** HABIT **Tiny, upright perennial**

IDENTIFICATION

Leaves are in three divisions, each part stalked and with two or three prominent lobes; light, glossy green. Flowers are minute, yellowy green; uniquely arranged in groups of five, with four around the top of the stem and one facing upwards. Fruits are in the same arrangement as flowers.

KEY FACT This plant has the alternative country name of Town-hall Clock, which very accurately describes the arrangement of the tiny flowers and subsequent fruits, with 'faces' in different directions around the top of the stalk.

STATUS AND COMMENTS

Found throughout Britain, but is rare in, or absent from, N Scotland. It is very easily missed, even when growing in colonies.

SPOTTER'S CHART

LOCATION	DATE/TIME

FACT FILE SIZE Height to 1.5m HABITAT Woodlands rides and glades, shady banks, damp grassland FLOWERING PERIOD Jun–Aug HABIT Tall, delicate, upright perennial

IDENTIFICATION
Leaves are pinnate, up to 20cm long; leaflets are in opposite pairs, lanceolate, raggedly toothed. Flowers are shades of pink, in dense heads on several branches at top of stem. Fruit capsules have a feathery parachute when ripe. Stem is hairy towards base.

KEY FACT
Marsh Valerian is similar but smaller and less showy, with a creeping, rooting habit; it is found in wet places such as fens and marshes.

SPOTTER'S CHART

LOCATION	DATE/TIME

STATUS AND COMMENTS
Can be found throughout Britain, thriving where the conditions are damp. In drier places the plant is smaller and altogether less conspicuous.

HONEYSUCKLE
Lonicera periclymenum

SIZE Height to 6m **HABITAT** Woodland, hedgerows, banks **FLOWERING PERIOD** Jun–Sep
HABIT Tall, climbing, scrambling perennial

IDENTIFICATION
Leaves are oval, up to 7cm long; dark green above, paler beneath. Flowers are pinkish yellow, up to 5cm long, trumpet-shaped, with elongated, curling lips and protruding stamens; highly fragrant. Fruits are bright red berries. Stem is very tough and strong, becoming woody with age.

STATUS AND COMMENTS
Common and widespread throughout Britain in a wide variety of habitats, including sea cliffs. In some conditions it crawls rather than climbs.

KEY FACT
The glorious heady scent of Honeysuckle flowers, usually strongest in the evening, attracts human as well as insect admirers. Old specimens can be very tall and spreading, with immensely tough stems.

SPOTTER'S CHART

LOCATION	DATE/TIME

FACT FILE

SIZE Height to 2m HABITAT Disturbed and waste ground, hedgerows, woods, banks FLOWERING PERIOD Jul–Aug HABIT Upright, very prickly biennial

IDENTIFICATION

Leaves are strap-like, spiny; they form a basal rosette in first year, which withers in second year and is replaced by opposite, fused stem leaves.

KEY FACT Where the leaves join the stem, there is often a 'cup' that fills with rainwater and dew. Birds drink from this sometimes, occasionally puncturing the 'cup' from below to get at the water.

Flowers are minute, pinkish purple; in spiny, egg-shaped heads 6–8cm long; heads are carried on tall, spiny stems.

STATUS AND COMMENTS

Common and widespread throughout Britain, except in Scotland, Wild Teasel often forms extensive, dense stands on suitable disturbed ground.

SPOTTER'S CHART	
LOCATION	DATE/TIME

SMALL TEASEL
Dipsacus pilosus

FACT FILE

SIZE Height to 1.2m **HABITAT** Woodland margins, hedgerows, banks; usually on damp calcareous soils
FLOWERING PERIOD Jul–Sep **HABIT** Upright, prickly biennial

IDENTIFICATION
Leaves are oval; basal leaves form a rosette. Flowers are small, white; in spiny, rather globular heads 15–20mm across (very different from those of Wild Teasel). Fruits are dry and carried in the dried, persisting flower heads. The whole plant is much less robust than Wild Teasel.

KEY FACT
Small Teasel seeds need to be disturbed before they will germinate, like those of its larger relative Wild Teasel; they will lie dormant if rank vegetation takes over its growing site.

STATUS AND COMMENTS
Rather local, with its main range centred on the English–Welsh border counties, central-S England and parts of East Anglia; only scattered records in central and N England; absent from W Britain and Scotland.

SPOTTER'S CHART

LOCATION	DATE/TIME

NETTLE-LEAVED BELLFLOWER
Campanula trachelium

FACT FILE

SIZE Height to 1m HABITAT Woodland,
hedgerows, scrub FLOWERING PERIOD Jul–Sep
HABIT Tall, erect, leafy, hairy perennial

IDENTIFICATION

Leaves are of two sorts:
lower leaves are heart-
shaped, toothed, on long
stalks; upper ones are oval,
toothed, on short stalks, and
very like Common Nettle
leaves. Flowers are violet-
blue, up to 4cm long, bell-shaped.
Fruits are brown capsules. Stem
is sharply angled.

KEY FACT

Giant Bellflower
resembles Nettle-leaved Bellflower
and is found in similar habitats, but
it has bigger flowers (up to 5cm long)
and a bluntly angled stem. It is found in
central and N England and S Scotland.

SPOTTER'S CHART

LOCATION	DATE/TIME

STATUS AND COMMENTS

Most common in S and E England,
found only locally in the W and
Wales, and uncommon or absent
in the N and Scotland.

OXEYE DAISY
Leucanthemum vulgare

FACT FILE

SIZE **Height to 75cm** HABITAT **Banks, verges, grassland, disturbed ground** FLOWERING PERIOD **May–Sep** HABIT **Upright perennial**

IDENTIFICATION
Leaves are of two sorts: stem leaves are small, deeply lobed, unstalked; basal leaves are larger, long-stalked, spoon-shaped, toothed, and form a rosette. Flowers are pure white florets, with a central disc of yellow florets, up to 5cm across.

KEY FACT Also known as Moon Daisy, the Oxeye Daisy has spread along many of our motorways and trunk roads, where its cheerful, bright flowers sometimes form sheets of colour. The flowers are very attractive to insects.

STATUS AND COMMENTS
Widespread and generally common throughout most of England and Wales in suitable habitats; patchily distributed in Scotland, and scarce in Highland regions and the NW.

SPOTTER'S CHART

LOCATION	DATE/TIME

SCENTLESS MAYWEED
Tripleurospermum inodorum

SIZE Height to 65cm **HABITAT** Verges, disturbed ground, cultivated soils **FLOWERING PERIOD** Apr–Oct **HABIT** Upright perennial

KEY FACT
Scentless Mayweed thrives on disturbance and often appears in abundance on newly created verges. Its flowers are attractive to butterflies and a wide range of other insects.

IDENTIFICATION
Leaves are finely divided and feathery, quite different from those of the superficially similar Oxeye Daisy. Flower heads are 20–35mm across, with yellow central florets surrounded by radiating white florets; flower heads are carried on long stalks. Fruits are papery. Scentless and hairless plant.

STATUS AND COMMENTS
Widespread and generally common to locally abundant in England and Wales, except in upland regions; in Scotland, mainly confined to lowlands in the S and E.

SPOTTER'S CHART

LOCATION	DATE/TIME

YARROW
Achillea millefolium

FACT FILE

SIZE Height to 45cm **HABITAT** Hedgerows, verges, banks, grassland, waste ground **FLOWERING PERIOD** Jun–Oct **HABIT** Upright perennial

IDENTIFICATION
Leaves are finely divided, feathery and fern-like, dark green; thickest at base, where they form a rosette. Flowers comprise yellowish central florets surrounded by white florets, up to 6mm across; they grow in flat heads up to 4cm across at top of stems. The plant has a sharp, astringent scent.

KEY FACT

Yarrow is tough and has deep roots, enabling it to survive in unpromising places; it can also survive repeated mowing, as mower blades tend to pass above its ground-hugging rosette.

STATUS AND COMMENTS
One of Britain's most widespread plants, and generally common throughout England, Wales and Scotland; found in a wide range of habitats and at most altitudes.

SPOTTER'S CHART

LOCATION	DATE/TIME

FACT FILE   SIZE Height to 45cm HABITAT Hedgerows, verges, disturbed ground, gardens FLOWERING PERIOD Jul–Aug HABIT Upright perennial

IDENTIFICATION

Leaves are deeply divided, Parsley-like in form, pale green. Flowers are daisy-like, 15–20mm across, with central yellow florets surrounded by radiating white florets; often borne in profusion in groups at top of stems. The whole plant is sharply, cleanly aromatic.

KEY FACT   Feverfew is an attractive plant with a long history as a medicinal herb. It was used for a variety of complaints and conditions, and is still a herbal remedy for headaches and migraines.

STATUS AND COMMENTS

Commonest near towns and villages, as it is an introduced plant that has escaped from gardens. It is absent from much of central and N Scotland.

SPOTTER'S CHART

LOCATION	DATE/TIME

HEMP-AGRIMONY
Eupatorium cannabinum

FACT FILE

SIZE Height to 1.5m **HABITAT** Woodland, damp hedgerows and ditches, stream-sides **FLOWERING PERIOD** Jul–Sep **HABIT** Tall, imposing perennial

KEY FACT A well-established Hemp-agrimony plant creates a large ball of dense, fibrous roots that is almost impenetrable (and very difficult to dig up!).

IDENTIFICATION
Leaves are trifoliate, each leaflet up to 10cm long, lanceolate, toothed; leaves are all opposite each other. Flowers are pink to purple; in dense, clustered heads at top of stems. Feathery/fluffy seeds are produced in abundance. Stem is reddish and downy.

STATUS AND COMMENTS
Widespread throughout much of Britain, but rare or absent from N Scotland. It has a preference for damp conditions, but can establish itself in much drier soils.

SPOTTER'S CHART

LOCATION	DATE/TIME

SIZE **Height to 30cm** HABITAT **Woodland, damp hedgerows and ditches, stream-sides** FLOWERING PERIOD **Mar–May** HABIT **Creeping, colony-forming perennial**

IDENTIFICATION

Leaves are large (up to 75cm across), heart-shaped, deeply veined; green, tinged red. Flowers are pinkish red; in tight clusters on a stout stem that appears before leaves and is covered in ribbon-like scales.

KEY FACT Closely related and similar to Butterbur is Winter Heliotrope. It is smaller, and its flowers, which appear from Dec to Mar, are vanilla-scented.

SPOTTER'S CHART

LOCATION	DATE/TIME

STATUS AND COMMENTS

Widespread throughout much of Britain, but absent from N Scotland. This strange-looking plant can form very large patches in favourable conditions.

MUGWORT
Artemisia vulgaris

FACT FILE

SIZE Height to 1.25m **HABITAT** Waste places, hedgerows, verges, banks **FLOWERING PERIOD** Jul–Sep **HABIT** Tall, many-branched perennial

KEY FACT
With an unappealing name and an unpromising appearance, Mugwort has few fans these days, but it was once used as a substitute for tea and tobacco, and as an ingredient in beer. Rub the leaves to enjoy the pleasant scent.

IDENTIFICATION
Leaves are pinnate, up to 10cm long; dark olive-green above, silvery beneath and covered with fine white hairs; lower leaves are stalked, upper ones unstalked. Flowers are tiny, brownish red; in tight groups clustered towards end of branching flower stems. Stem is reddish. The plant is faintly, sweetly aromatic.

STATUS AND COMMENTS
Found throughout Britain except in the wildest and highest places.

SPOTTER'S CHART

LOCATION	DATE/TIME

SIZE Height to 75cm **HABITAT** Waste places, hedgerows, verges, banks **FLOWERING PERIOD** Jul–Sep **HABIT** Medium-sized, many-branched perennial

IDENTIFICATION
Leaves are pinnate, up to 5cm long, bluntly cut; olive-green, both surfaces covered with fine white hairs. Flowers are tiny, yellow; in tight groups clustered towards end of branching flower stems. The plant is powerfully, very noticeably aromatic.

STATUS AND COMMENTS
Found in many parts of Britain except N Scotland and higher, wilder regions. The very similar Sea Wormwood grows on sea walls and the edges of saltmarshes.

KEY FACT
With such a pungent aroma, it is no surprise that Wormwood was once used for medicinal purposes. As so often with plants, the clue is in the name: it was used to purge intestinal worms.

SPOTTER'S CHART

LOCATION	DATE/TIME

COLT'S-FOOT
Tussilago farfara

FACT FILE

SIZE Height to 20cm **HABITAT** Banks, verges, waste places, bare ground **FLOWERING PERIOD** Feb–Apr
HABIT Low, creeping, woolly perennial

IDENTIFICATION
Leaves appear after flowers; heart-shaped to round, toothed, with a pointed tip, up to 20cm across; dark green above, furry and white beneath. Flowers are bright yellow, daisy-like, up to 35mm across; at top of a scaly, leafless purple-green stem. Fruits are small, oblong seeds with 'parachutes' attached.

KEY FACT The cheerful flowers of Colt's-foot brighten early spring days, but they close up when the sun goes in. The seedhead is very similar to a Dandelion 'clock'.

STATUS AND COMMENTS
Common throughout Britain in its preferred habitats, which include disturbed ground and such places as cliffs where the soil is crumbly or moving. It prefers clay soils.

SPOTTER'S CHART

LOCATION	DATE/TIME

COMMON RAGWORT
Senecio jacobaea

FACT FILE
SIZE Height to 1.25m HABITAT Waste ground, verges, banks, grassland FLOWERING PERIOD Jun–Oct HABIT Upright, medium-tall biennial or perennial

KEY FACT Grazing livestock avoid the living poisonous plant, but if it is accidentally harvested and gets into hay it becomes undetectable and can then kill the animals that eat it.

IDENTIFICATION
Leaves are pinnate, with many divisions and rounded lobes; dark green above, lighter beneath; lower leaves stalked, upper ones unstalked. Flowers are yellow, daisy-like; in tight, flat-headed clusters at top of flowering stems. Fruits are small seeds with 'parachutes' attached. The plant is poisonous.

STATUS AND COMMENTS
Found throughout Britain, Common Ragwort is a familiar plant of waste ground and poorly managed grazing lands, and is especially noticeable in such places because grazing animals will not eat it.

SPOTTER'S CHART

LOCATION	DATE/TIME

OXFORD RAGWORT
Senecio squalidus

FACT FILE

SIZE Height to 50cm HABITAT Waste and derelict ground, verges, railway embankments and sidings FLOWERING PERIOD Apr–Nov HABIT Untidy, sprawling annual or perennial

KEY FACT Oxford Ragwort has a famous distribution story: it escaped from Oxford Botanic Garden in the 1800s and subsequently began a remarkable colonisation of Britain via the growing railway network, with innumerable feathery seeds carried along in the wake of the newfangled steam trains.

IDENTIFICATION
Leaves are pinnate, with many divisions and pointed lobes, making it look ragged; lower leaves are stalked, upper ones unstalked. Flowers are yellow, daisy-like, up to 25mm across; in loose groups at top of flowering stems. Fruits are small seeds with 'parachutes' attached.

SPOTTER'S CHART

LOCATION	DATE/TIME

STATUS AND COMMENTS
Found throughout Britain, frequently in man-made or industrialised settings.

FACT FILE SIZE Height to 1.25m HABITAT Woodland edges and rides, hedgerows, wasteland FLOWERING PERIOD Jul–Sep HABIT Tall, erect, hairy biennial

IDENTIFICATION
Leaves are large (up to 40cm long), heart-shaped, but longer than they are wide; dark green above, downy beneath. Flowers are purple, tiny; in a tight group crowning an egg-shaped flower head that is covered in hooked bracts (the burs). Stem is reddish, woolly and branched.

KEY FACT Anyone who has had burdock burs stuck in their clothes or hair knows that they stick fast, and are a remarkably efficient way for the plants to spread their seeds from place to place.

STATUS AND COMMENTS
Found throughout Britain, except in N Scotland. The very similar Greater Burdock is restricted to S England and Wales; its leaves are as wide as they are long.

SPOTTER'S CHART

LOCATION	DATE/TIME

SPEAR THISTLE
Cirsium vulgare

FACT FILE

SIZE Height to 1m HABITAT Waste ground, hedgerows, grassland, disturbed ground FLOWERING PERIOD Jul–Sep HABIT Upright, spiny biennial

IDENTIFICATION
Leaves are pinnate, wavy, lobed, toothed, and very spiny. Flowers are purple, fragrant, up to 4cm across, with tightly packed florets emerging from a spherical, extremely spiny base. Fruits have feathery white hairs for wind dispersal. Stems are downy and covered with spines.

KEY FACT The similar Creeping Thistle does not have spiny stems, and its smaller flowers are pale pink, unlike the Spear Thistle's purple flowers.

STATUS AND COMMENTS
Widespread and common throughout most of England, Wales and Scotland, but not so common in the Scottish Highlands. The fragrant flowers attract insects such as butterflies.

SPOTTER'S CHART

LOCATION	DATE/TIME

CREEPING THISTLE
Cirsium arvense

SIZE Height to 90cm HABITAT Disturbed grassland, verges, waysides FLOWERING PERIOD Jun–Sep HABIT Upright, spreading perennial

IDENTIFICATION
Leaves are pinnate, with spiny lobes; wavy. Flowers are lilac-pink, in tightly packed heads up to 15mm across; heads are in clusters at top of flowering stems, which lack spines. Fruits have feathery hairs to aid wind dispersal of seeds and are produced in profusion.

KEY FACT As well as spreading by means of clouds of feathery seeds, Creeping Thistle has tenacious creeping roots that send up shoots from which new thistles grow, making the plant a pest in fields and gardens.

STATUS AND COMMENTS
Widespread and generally extremely common throughout much of England, Wales and Scotland, but scarce in, or absent from, parts of the Highlands and NW Scotland.

SPOTTER'S CHART

LOCATION	DATE/TIME

MARSH THISTLE
Cirsium palustre

FACT FILE

SIZE Height to 1.3m **HABITAT** Woodland clearings and glades, grassland; prefers damp conditions
FLOWERING PERIOD Jul–Sep **HABIT** Upright, hairy biennial

KEY FACT

Marsh Thistle's winged and spiny stems differentiate it from Creeping Thistle, and its flowers are darker than those of either Creeping Thistle or Spear Thistle.

IDENTIFICATION
Leaves are narrow, pinnate, edges covered in spines. Flowers are reddish purple, in tightly packed heads up to 16mm across; heads are in clusters at top of stem. Fruits have feathery hairs to aid wind dispersal of seeds. Stems are winged and spiny, and often flushed purple.

STATUS AND COMMENTS
Widespread and generally extremely common throughout much of England, Wales and Scotland, Marsh Thistle thrives only in damp conditions, and is absent from dry soils.

SPOTTER'S CHART

LOCATION	DATE/TIME

FACT FILE

SIZE **Height to 1m** HABITAT **Hedgerows, banks, verges, grassy places** FLOWERING PERIOD **Jun–Sep** HABIT **Upright, hairy perennial**

IDENTIFICATION

Leaves are narrow, lanceolate, toothed; lower leaves are stalked, upper unstalked. Flowers are pale reddish-purple florets, in a tight group crowning a hard, spherical flower head that has dark bracts. Fruits are brown seeds. Stem is grooved.

STATUS AND COMMENTS

Still often known as Hardheads and sometimes as Black Knapweed, Common Knapweed is common throughout Britain in dry habitats.

KEY FACT

The leaves of Common Knapweed are different from those of the very similar Greater Knapweed: those of Common Knapweed are clearly lance-shaped, while Greater Knapweed's are complex and deeply cut.

SPOTTER'S CHART

LOCATION	DATE/TIME

GREATER KNAPWEED
Centaurea scabiosa

FACT FILE

SIZE Height to 1m **HABITAT** Banks, hedgerows, verges, grassland, cliffs; prefers calcareous soils
FLOWERING PERIOD Jun–Sep **HABIT** Upright perennial

IDENTIFICATION
Leaves are pinnate, rounded, deeply lobed; lower leaves are stalked, upper ones unstalked. Flower are bright reddish-purple florets in heads up to 5cm across; inner florets are tightly packed, the outer ones long and spreading. Flower heads have a swollen base, are solitary and are carried on long stems.

KEY FACT
Greater Knapweed has a more restricted distribution than Common Knapweed, and its flower heads are more showy, with more spreading florets.

SPOTTER'S CHART

LOCATION	DATE/TIME

STATUS AND COMMENTS
Widespread and locally common on suitable soils in central and **S** England, and least numerous in the **SW**; mostly coastal in Wales; locally common in **N** England; rare and local in Scotland. A classic downland plant.

FACT FILE   SIZE Height to 1.25m HABITAT Banks, verges, grassy places; prefers calcareous soils FLOWERING PERIOD Jun–Sep
HABIT Upright, branched perennial

IDENTIFICATION
Leaves are narrow, lanceolate, toothed and/or lobed; lower leaves are larger and stalked, upper ones unstalked. Flowers are bright, light blue florets in heads up to 4cm across; heads are ranged along upper stems, often appearing in profusion. Stem is grooved and hairy.

STATUS AND COMMENTS
Still quite common in parts of S England, especially on chalky soils, but rare or absent elsewhere in Britain.

KEY FACT

The vivid blue flowers of Chicory make it look exotic for the English countryside, and so it is, having been introduced long ago as a foodplant. Latterly, its roasted roots have been used a substitute for coffee.

SPOTTER'S CHART

LOCATION	DATE/TIME

GOAT'S-BEARD
Tragopogon pratensis

FACT FILE

SIZE Height to 70cm **HABITAT** Banks, verges, hedgerows, waste ground **FLOWERING PERIOD** May–Aug
HABIT Upright annual or perennial

IDENTIFICATION
Leaves are long, narrow, undulating, strappy and grass-like; pale, shiny green. Flowers are yellow florets in heads up to 4cm across; behind them are distinctive long green bracts.
Fruits are large, feathery 'clocks'.

STATUS AND COMMENTS
Relatively common in parts of England and Wales, but rare or absent from much of Scotland and mountainous regions.

KEY FACT

The flowers close on dull days and before midday (hence its common country name of Jack-go-to-bed-at-noon), when it may easily be taken for a grass. It has a much larger and more splendid 'clock' than Dandelion.

SPOTTER'S CHART

LOCATION	DATE/TIME

SMOOTH SOW-THISTLE
Sonchus oleraceus

FACT FILE

SIZE Height to 1.5m **HABITAT** Waste and disturbed ground; gardens **FLOWERING PERIOD** May–Nov **HABIT** Upright annual or biennial

IDENTIFICATION

Leaves are pinnate, toothed, with triangular, softly spiny lobes; matt green; they clasp the stem. Flowers are pale yellow florets, in heads up to 25mm across; heads are in clusters at top of stem. Fruits are small, feathery 'clocks'. Stem is winged, and exudes white sap if broken.

KEY FACT

Prickly Sow-thistle is very similar, but has wrinkled, very sharp and spiny, double-toothed leaf margins, shiny upper leaves, and darker flowers. It grows in much the same places as Smooth Sow-thistle.

STATUS AND COMMENTS

Very common throughout Britain, but very much a plant of man-made or disturbed habitats.

SPOTTER'S CHART

LOCATION	DATE/TIME

PERENNIAL SOW-THISTLE
Sonchus arvensis

FACT FILE

SIZE Height to 2m HABITAT Waste and disturbed
ground, grassland, verges FLOWERING PERIOD Jul–Oct
HABIT Tall, upright perennial

KEY FACT Like many of its family, Perennial Sow-thistle can
spread by means of creeping rhizomes, and is often seen in clumps.

IDENTIFICATION
Leaves are long and narrow, with pinnate lobes and soft spines on leaf
edges; shiny green above, pale beneath: they clasp the stem. Flowers are
deep yellow florets, in heads up
to 5cm across; heads are in
clusters at top of stem. Fruits
form feathery 'clocks'. Stem is
grooved, hairy, and exudes white
sap if broken.

SPOTTER'S CHART

LOCATION	DATE/TIME

STATUS AND COMMENTS
Found throughout Britain. Like its
close relatives Smooth and Prickly
sow-thistle, it is a plant of disturbed
ground, as well as being found in
grassland, copses and woodland.

PRICKLY LETTUCE
Lactuca serriola

FACT FILE SIZE Height to 1.5m HABITAT Grassy areas, verges, waste ground FLOWERING PERIOD Jul–Sep HABIT Tall, upright biennial

IDENTIFICATION

Leaves are oblong, grey-green, with soft spines on leaf edges and bristles on lower midrib; they clasp the stem and are held vertically. Flowers are yellow florets, in heads up to 12mm across; heads are in loose groups at top of stem. Fruits have a small 'parachute'. Stem is prickly and exudes a smelly white sap if broken.

KEY FACT

A very similar relative is Great Lettuce, which is taller and holds its leaves horizontally. Both are distant relatives of Cultivated Lettuce but are inedible.

STATUS AND COMMENTS

Locally common in parts of S and E England, Prickly Lettuce is uncommon or absent from the rest of Britain.

SPOTTER'S CHART

LOCATION	DATE/TIME

COMMON DANDELION
Taraxacum officinale

SIZE **Height to 30cm** HABITAT **Grasslands, verges, banks, hedgerows, waste ground, gardens**
FLOWERING PERIOD **Mar–Oct** HABIT **Upright perennial**

IDENTIFICATION
Leaves are narrowly oval, with sharp triangular lobes and a prominently ribbed central vein; they form a rosette. Flowers are yellow florets, in tightly packed heads up to 5cm across; heads are solitary and carried on hollow stems. Fruits are spherical heads ('clocks') of seeds with feathery hairs that aid wind dispersal.

KEY FACT
One of Britain's most common wild plants, Dandelion has many uses: its young leaves can be eaten in salads, its flowers turned into wine, and its roots roasted as a coffee substitute.

STATUS AND COMMENTS
Widespread and generally common throughout England, Wales and Scotland, and with very many recognisably but subtly different forms (microspecies) adapted to the range of British habitats.

SPOTTER'S CHART

LOCATION	DATE/TIME

NIPPLEWORT
Lapsana communis

FACT FILE

SIZE **Height to 90cm** HABITAT **Grassy areas, hedgerows, verges, disturbed and waste ground**
FLOWERING PERIOD **Jul–Oct** HABIT **Upright, thin-branched annual**

IDENTIFICATION

Leaves are oval to lanceolate, blunt-toothed, dark green; lower leaves have pronounced lobes towards base. Flowers are yellow florets, in small heads carried in clusters. Fruits are small brown capsules. The plant often appears 'leggy', with the flowers at the ends of long, leafless stems.

STATUS AND COMMENTS

Common throughout Britain, and a familiar garden weed on light soils.

KEY FACT

Once used both as a salad ingredient and as a medicine, Nipplewort is more likely these days to be enjoyed by chickens, which are particularly fond of it.

SPOTTER'S CHART

LOCATION	DATE/TIME

MOUSE-EAR HAWKWEED
Pilosella officinarum

FACT FILE

SIZE Height to 30cm **HABITAT** Grassy areas, heaths, verges, banks **FLOWERING PERIOD** Jun–Oct **HABIT** Creeping perennial

IDENTIFICATION
Leaves are narrowly oval, blunt-ended; darker above and with random white hairs, lighter and furry below; lower leaves form a basal rosette, from which runners extend. Flowers are yellow florets with bright red stripes underneath. The single flower heads are on leafless, hairy stems.

KEY FACT

A close relative of Mouse-ear Hawkweed has an even more enchanting name: Fox-and-cubs. It is a garden escape with distinctive burnt-orange flowers in a cluster at the top of the stem.

STATUS AND COMMENTS
Common throughout Britain. Although it shares a common name with other hawkweeds, it is not related to them.

SPOTTER'S CHART

LOCATION	DATE/TIME

HAWKWEEDS
Hieracium spp.

FACT FILE
SIZE Height 25cm–1m+ HABITAT Woodland glades and rides, hedgerows, banks, verges, grassy places
FLOWERING PERIOD Jun–Oct HABIT Variable upright perennials

IDENTIFICATION
The 200-plus hawkweed in Britain are virtually identical; following is a generic description. Leaves are lanceolate, toothed, pointed at tip, hairy beneath. Flowers are yellow florets in heads; heads are in clusters on hairy stems. Some hawkweeds have a basal rosette of leaves, and some are more leafy than others.

KEY FACT Even experts can find it tricky to differentiate the many hawkweeds in Britain, so the description here covers the group generally.

STATUS AND COMMENTS
Common throughout much of Britain. To make themselves even more fascinating and complex, hawkweeds form seeds without pollination, and the many different forms do not cross-breed.

SPOTTER'S CHART

LOCATION	DATE/TIME

BRISTLY OXTONGUE
Picris echioides

FACT FILE

SIZE **Height to 90cm** HABITAT **Grassy and waste places, roadsides, verges** FLOWERING PERIOD **Jun–Oct** HABIT **Upright, branched, bristly annual or biennial**

KEY FACT Hawkweed Oxtongue is very like Bristly Oxtongue and grows in similar places, but it has thinner leaves and its bristles do not have swollen bases.

IDENTIFICATION
Leaves are oblong, wavy, pointed at tip, covered in bristles with swollen bases; upper leaves are unstalked and clasp stem. Flowers are yellow florets, in heads up to 20mm across; heads are in loose clusters on bristly stems. The entire plant is covered in bristles.

STATUS AND COMMENTS
Found only in **S Britain**, where it is common in some areas and absent from others.

SPOTTER'S CHART

LOCATION	DATE/TIME

AUTUMN HAWKBIT
Leontodon autumnalis

SIZE **Height to 20cm** HABITAT **Grassy and waste places, roadsides, verges** FLOWERING PERIOD **Jun–Oct** HABIT **Upright perennial**

KEY FACT
Two other similar hawkbits that may be found are Rough Hawkbit, with hairy stems and very hairy leaves; and Lesser Hawkbit, which is less hairy than Rough Hawkbit and usually does not have branching flower heads.

IDENTIFICATION
Leaves are long, pinnate, deeply lobed, all growing from a basal rosette. Flowers are yellow florets in heads up to 20mm across; heads are on separate branching stems. Fruits are Dandelion-like 'clocks'. The whole plant is rather Dandelion-like.

STATUS AND COMMENTS
Common throughout Britain.

SPOTTER'S CHART

LOCATION	DATE/TIME

CAT'S-EAR
Hypochaeris radicata

SIZE Height to 45cm **HABITAT** Grassland, meadows, verges; commonest on acid soils **FLOWERING PERIOD** Jun–Sep
HABIT Upright perennial

KEY FACT

Unlike the superficially similar Dandelion, Cat's-ear has wiry (not hollow), branched flower stems and hairy (not smooth) leaves.

IDENTIFICATION
Leaves are lanceolate, bristly, with wavy edges; all growing from a basal rosette. Flower heads are up to 4cm across, with rich yellow florets; heads are solitary but flowering stems are branched. Fruits have small, feathery hairs.

STATUS AND COMMENTS
Widespread and generally common throughout most of England, Wales and Scotland; commonest on dry soils, and scarce in areas with high rainfall and waterlogged ground.

SPOTTER'S CHART

LOCATION	DATE/TIME

SMOOTH HAWK'S-BEARD
Crepis capillaris

FACT FILE   SIZE Height to 90cm HABITAT Grassland, heaths, roadsides, verges FLOWERING PERIOD Jun–Sep HABIT Erect, branching annual or biennial

IDENTIFICATION
Leaves are of two kinds: lower leaves are long, pinnate, lobed, forming a basal rosette; upper ones are smaller, clasping stems and with pointed bases. Flowers are tiny, bright yellow flower heads up to 15mm across, in small clusters on several stems.

STATUS AND COMMENTS
A common plant throughout Britain, and a familiar sight in dry, grassy places.

KEY FACT

Similar, but restricted to S England, is Rough Hawk's-beard. As its name implies, it is hairy (Smooth Hawk's-beard is not); it is also a much taller plant with significantly bigger flowers (up to 30mm across).

SPOTTER'S CHART

LOCATION	DATE/TIME

BLUEBELL
Hyacinthoides non-scripta

SIZE Height to 50cm **HABITAT** Woodlands, hedges, banks; also hillsides and cliffs, especially in the **W**
FLOWERING PERIOD Apr–Jun **HABIT** Upright bulbous perennial

IDENTIFICATION

Leaves are long, narrow, strap-like, glossy green; all grow from the base. Flowers are an unmistakable deep blue, bell-shaped, scented; individual bells all fall the same way on the stem. Frequently found in large colonies, and an indicator of ancient woodland sites.

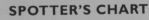

KEY FACT On warm, sunny days in spring, the combination of intense blue flowers and heady scent in a Bluebell wood can be almost hallucinatory. Pink or white colour variations can be naturally occurring.

STATUS AND COMMENTS

Common and widespread, and the quintessential British woodland plant. It is threatened in some areas by cross-breeding with the more vigorous Spanish Bluebell.

SPOTTER'S CHART

LOCATION	DATE/TIME

SPANISH BLUEBELL
Hyacinthoides hispanica

FACT FILE

SIZE **Height to 50cm** HABITAT **Woodlands, hedges, gardens** FLOWERING PERIOD **Apr–Jun** HABIT **Upright bulbous perennial**

KEY FACT Hybrids between Spanish Bluebell and native Bluebell are common, and the resultant plants may show characteristics of one, or both, parents, making identification difficult.

IDENTIFICATION

Leaves are long, strap-like, glossy green (significantly wider than those of the native Bluebell). Flowers are usually pale blue (occasionally pink or white), bell-shaped (without the turned-back tips that the native Bluebell has); bells fall on different sides of the stem (unlike the native Bluebell).

STATUS AND COMMENTS

Increasingly found in woods and hedges, and often cross-breeds with the native Bluebell. It is commonly grown in gardens, and frequently escapes.

SPOTTER'S CHART

LOCATION	DATE/TIME

RAMSONS
Allium ursinum

FACT FILE

SIZE Height to 40cm HABITAT Woodlands, hedges, shady banks FLOWERING PERIOD Apr–Jun
HABIT Upright bulbous perennial

IDENTIFICATION
Leaves are up to 20cm long, arrow-shaped, glossy green, curling towards tip; all grow from the base. Flowers are white, up to 15mm across, star-shaped, long-stemmed; they grow in circular clusters from top of the thin, leafless main stem. The plant is strongly aromatic.

KEY FACT Ramsons have the pungent aroma of garlic, to which they are closely related. The leaves are edible, but they can be confused with Lily-of-the-valley and Lords-and-ladies, both of which are poisonous.

STATUS AND COMMENTS
Locally common throughout Britain. In favourable conditions – usually deciduous woodlands – Ramsons can grow in great drifts, often to the exclusion of other plants.

SPOTTER'S CHART

LOCATION	DATE/TIME

FACT FILE

SIZE **Height to 40cm** HABITAT **Hedgerows, banks, walls; at its best in full sun** FLOWERING PERIOD **Feb–Jun** HABIT **Upright bulbous perennial**

KEY FACT

In sunny, sheltered situations Three-cornered Garlic (also called Three-cornered Leek) may flower very early in the year. It can spread rapidly, often creating drifts.

IDENTIFICATION

Leaves are long, narrow, flat or keeled; all grow from the base. Flowers are white with green stripes and bright yellow stamens; bell-shaped; they grow in drooping clusters from top of the three-cornered stem. Aromatic when rubbed.

STATUS AND COMMENTS

Locally common in SW England (but absent elsewhere), Three-cornered Garlic grows particularly well on the Isles of Scilly, where it thrives in the mild, sunny conditions.

SPOTTER'S CHART

LOCATION	DATE/TIME

WILD ONION
Allium vineale

SIZE Height to 60cm **HABITAT** Hedgerows, grassland, banks, verges, waste places **FLOWERING PERIOD** May–Jul **HABIT** Upright bulbous perennial

IDENTIFICATION
Leaves are long, thin, semicircular in section, dull green. Flowers are tiny, pinkish white; in small clusters at top of stem; they are usually accompanied on the flower head by tiny bulbs, or bulbils, which can grow into new plants. The flower head is at first protected by a green spathe that dries to a papery sheath.

STATUS AND COMMENTS
Common throughout S Britain but rarer in the N.

KEY FACT
The common names of wild flowers can be confusing, especially when the plant has more than one, as this one does. Whether you call it Wild Onion or Crow Garlic may depend on where you come from, or what your parents called it.

SPOTTER'S CHART

LOCATION	DATE/TIME

FACT FILE

SIZE **Height to 20cm** HABITAT **Woodland; prefers calcareous soils** FLOWERING PERIOD **May–Jul** HABIT **Creeping bulbous perennial**

IDENTIFICATION

Leaves are elongated oval, glossy green, growing from base of plant; usually two per plant. Flowers are white, bell-shaped, up to 6mm long, in a line all drooping one way on stem; very fragrant. Fruits are red berries. The plant is poisonous. It spreads by means of creeping rhizomes and can form carpets.

KEY FACT Britain has small native populations of Lily-of-the-valley, but this is the same plant grown in gardens, and it does occasionally escape.

SPOTTER'S CHART

LOCATION	DATE/TIME

STATUS AND COMMENTS

Restricted to woods in England; rare in Scotland and Wales.

COMMON SOLOMON'S-SEAL
Polygonatum multiflorum

FACT FILE

SIZE **Height to 80cm** HABITAT **Dry woodlands; prefers calcareous soils** FLOWERING PERIOD **May–Jun** HABIT **Upright, creeping perennial**

IDENTIFICATION
Leaves are oval, prominently veined, with a pointed tip; they grow along arched stems. Flowers are very small, greenish white, bell-shaped, waisted in middle; in groups of two or three along stem. Fruits are black berries. Stem is round. The plant spreads by means of creeping rhizomes and can form carpets.

STATUS AND COMMENTS
Found throughout Britain, but most common in the S.

KEY FACT

The very widespread Garden Solomon's-seal is a hybrid of Common Solomon's-seal and the uncommon native Angular Solomon's-seal. Garden Solomon's-seal has an angled (not round) stem; Angular Solomon's-seal has flowers that are not waisted.

SPOTTER'S CHART

LOCATION	DATE/TIME

HERB-PARIS
Paris quadrifolia

FACT FILE

SIZE **Height to 40cm** HABITAT **Damp woodlands;**
prefers calcareous soils FLOWERING PERIOD **May–Jun**
HABIT **Upright perennial**

IDENTIFICATION
Leaves are oval, broad, prominently veined, growing in a highly distinctive
whorl – usually of four leaves – at top of stem. Flowers are greenish, rayed,
tiny; unlike any other flower, they are solitary at centre of whorl of leaves.
Fruits are small black berries.

KEY FACT You are
unlikely to mistake Herb-Paris
for any other plant, as it is unique
in its appearance. It is, however,
patchily distributed and elusive.

STATUS AND COMMENTS
Locally common in parts of S,
central and N England, Herb-Paris
is absent from the far W of England,
and much of Wales and Scotland.

SPOTTER'S CHART

LOCATION	DATE/TIME

BUTCHER'S-BROOM
Ruscus aculeatus

SIZE **Height to 90cm** HABITAT **Dry, shady woodlands; prefers calcareous soils** FLOWERING PERIOD **Jan–Apr** HABIT **Upright, stiff, evergreen perennial**

IDENTIFICATION

Leaves are modified stems: flat, oval, stiff, dark green, up to 4cm long with a spiny tip. Flowers are tiny, greenish; they sit in centre of 'leaves'. Fruits are large, prominent, bright red berries that stay on the plant for a long time.

KEY FACT With its stiff, dark stems, peculiar 'leaves' and bright berries, Butcher's-broom is highly distinctive. Usually, male and female plants must grow together for berries to appear, but some garden forms are hermaphrodite (and may have larger berries).

STATUS AND COMMENTS

Locally common in parts of S England and Wales, Butcher's-broom has escaped from gardens in other parts of Britain.

SPOTTER'S CHART

LOCATION	DATE/TIME

WILD DAFFODIL
Narcissus pseudonarcissus

FACT FILE

SIZE **Height to 40cm** HABITAT **Open woodland, hedgerows, meadows, banks** FLOWERING PERIOD **Feb–Apr** HABIT **Bulbous perennial**

IDENTIFICATION
Leaves are long, narrow, arising from base; grey-green. Flowers are the familiar daffodil shape: six wavy, pale yellow petals surrounding a golden-yellow trumpet; up to 6cm across; held horizontally or slightly drooping on flower stalk.

KEY FACT
There are, of course, hundreds of cultivated forms of daffodil, some of them similar to the original Wild Daffodil. The location, and the combination of pale and bright yellows in the flowers, can be a clue to a genuine wild population.

STATUS AND COMMENTS
Locally common throughout England, where they are more often found in the S and W. Rare in Scotland. They prefer slightly acid soils.

SPOTTER'S CHART

LOCATION	DATE/TIME

SNOWDROP
Galanthus nivalis

FACT FILE

SIZE **Height to 25cm** HABITAT **Damp woodland and clearings, meadows, banks** FLOWERING PERIOD **Jan–Mar** HABIT **Bulbous perennial**

IDENTIFICATION
Leaves are narrow, upright, arising from base; grey-green. Flowers are white, drooping, with three pure white outer sepals and three shorter inner petals that are tipped with green. Fruits are small capsules.

STATUS AND COMMENTS
Snowdrops can be found growing throughout Britain. They are so often planted and just as often naturalised that no one knows what their original natural distribution might have been.

KEY FACT
Perhaps the most welcome first sign of spring, Snowdrops come in numerous species and cultivars, and can flower in the hardest weather. They frequently grow in wonderful white drifts, but whether they are natural or planted is often mysterious.

SPOTTER'S CHART

LOCATION	DATE/TIME

STINKING IRIS
Iris foetidissima

FACT FILE

SIZE **Height to 75cm** HABITAT **Woodlands, banks, hedgerows, sea cliffs; prefers calcareous soils**
FLOWERING PERIOD **Mar–Jul** HABIT **Upright, stiff perennial**

IDENTIFICATION

Leaves are strap-like, sharp-edged, with a pointed tip; shiny green when young, leathery when old. Flowers are purplish and yellow: outer parts are pale but heavily veined with purple, inner parts are pale yellow. Fruits are pods; green at first, ripening and opening to reveal bright orange berries.

KEY FACT This is one of the many plants whose reputation for having a nasty smell is much exaggerated. It does have a distinctive smell, which some liken to roast beef.

STATUS AND COMMENTS

Naturally locally common in S Britain, Stinking Iris has been introduced elsewhere.

SPOTTER'S CHART

LOCATION	DATE/TIME

BLACK BRYONY
Tamus communis

SIZE **Height to 3m** HABITAT **Woodland edges,
hedgerows, waste places** FLOWERING PERIOD **May–Jul**
HABIT **Climbing, twining perennial**

IDENTIFICATION
Leaves are large (up to 10cm long and wide), heart-shaped, bright green, and with a prominent network of veins. Flowers are tiny, very pale whitish green, with six petals; they grow on short flowering spikes. Fruits are red berries, often produced in large numbers; poisonous. Twines clockwise; does not have tendrils.

KEY FACT Black Bryony is similar to the unrelated White Bryony, but the leaves of that species are very lobed, it has coiled tendrils, and its flowers have only five petals.

STATUS AND COMMENTS
Common in S Britain, but absent or rare further N.

SPOTTER'S CHART

LOCATION	DATE/TIME

LORDS-AND-LADIES
Arum maculatum

SIZE **Height to 50cm** HABITAT **Woodland, hedgerows, waste places; prefers calcareous soils** FLOWERING PERIOD **Apr–May** HABIT **Upright, very distinctive, perennial**

IDENTIFICATION

Leaves are arrow-shaped, glossy, wrinkly, often with a patterning of brown splodges. Flower structure is highly distinctive: a green (becoming brown) cloak-like spathe partly surrounds a purple-brown rod (the spadix), hidden at the base of which are minute male and female flowers. Fruits are groups of highly poisonous red berries.

KEY FACT The poisonous berries can kill if they are eaten. Italian Lords-and-ladies is a less common relative with bigger, unwrinkled and unspotted leaves (marbled or otherwise variegated in some forms), and a yellow spadix.

STATUS AND COMMENTS

Common in S Britain, but uncommon in N Scotland.

SPOTTER'S CHART

LOCATION	DATE/TIME

LADY ORCHID
Orchis purpurea

FACT FILE

SIZE Height to 80cm **HABITAT** Open woodland, banks, scrub; usually on calcareous soils **FLOWERING PERIOD** Apr–May **HABIT** Upright perennial

IDENTIFICATION
Leaves are oval with a pointed tip, shiny green; broader at base of plant, where they form a rosette; a few narrower leaves partly sheathe flowering stem. Flower spike is a spectacular cluster of flowers with purple-brown 'bonnets' and paler, spotted 'bodies'.

KEY FACT Look closely at the beautiful flower spike – if you are lucky enough to find one – and you'll see why it's called Lady Orchid: each flower has a 'bonneted' head, below which is a lip resembling a person in a spotted dress. The plant is delicately scented.

STATUS AND COMMENTS
Virtually confined to Kent, and very occasionally growing elsewhere in the S.

SPOTTER'S CHART

LOCATION	DATE/TIME

EARLY PURPLE ORCHID
Orchis mascula

FACT FILE

SIZE **Height to 50cm** HABITAT **Open woodland, grassland, scrub; usually on calcareous soils**
FLOWERING PERIOD **Apr–Jun** HABIT **Upright perennial**

KEY FACT

Like some other orchids, Early Purple Orchid is variable in its appearance: the flowers can range from white through to deep purple, and the leaves may or may not be spotted. Even the scent varies: from sweet to something approaching rank.

IDENTIFICATION
Leaves are rounded oblong, glossy green, usually (but not always) with prominent purplish blotches; they form a rosette. Flower spike is a loose cluster of flowers with pinkish-purple petals; the three-lobed lower petal or lip has small purple spots.

STATUS AND COMMENTS
Common through much of Britain, Early Purple Orchid is one of our most familiar orchids.

SPOTTER'S CHART

LOCATION	DATE/TIME

GREEN-WINGED ORCHID
Anacamptis morio

FACT FILE

SIZE Height to 30cm **HABITAT** Damp meadows, occasionally banks and lawns **FLOWERING PERIOD** Apr–Jun **HABIT** Upright perennial

IDENTIFICATION
Leaves are extended oblong, glossy green; they form a rosette, a few partly sheathing the flowering spike. Flower spike is a stubby cluster of flowers that ends abruptly. Individual flowers vary in colour from white through to deep purple and are unscented.

STATUS AND COMMENTS
Locally common, but with a patchy distribution, in lowland England and Wales; rare in Scotland.

KEY FACT
Green-winged Orchids can pop up, unannounced, in meadows or lawns, sometimes in huge numbers. Very often this happens when grassland is uncut or unmanaged for a period.

SPOTTER'S CHART

LOCATION	DATE/TIME

FACT FILE   SIZE **Height to 40cm** HABITAT **Woodland clearings and rides, scrub, grassy banks** FLOWERING PERIOD **May–Jun** HABIT **Upright perennial**

IDENTIFICATION

Leaves are oblong, leathery green, prominently veined. Flower spike is tall, with a scattering of flowers. Individual flowers (the 'flies') are chocolatey purple, with a blue patch on 'abdomen'; they look very like insects, complete with antennae, wings, and even two dots for eyes.

KEY FACT   Fly Orchids merge with the vegetation around them and are tricky to see, but it is well worth searching them out. And the insect impersonation works: the males of certain small wasp species try to mate with the flowers, collecting and dispersing pollen in the process.

STATUS AND COMMENTS

Locally common in England and Wales; but absent from Scotland.

SPOTTER'S CHART

LOCATION	DATE/TIME

COMMON SPOTTED-ORCHID
Dactylorhiza fuchsii

FACT FILE

SIZE **Height to 60cm** HABITAT **Open woodland, hedgerows, banks, verges, grassland** FLOWERING PERIOD **May–Aug** HABIT **Upright perennial**

KEY FACT
Common Spotted-orchids are very variable in flower colour. To add to the identification challenge, they hybridise very easily with similar orchid species, but the three-lobed lip with a slightly longer central lobe is a good clue.

IDENTIFICATION
Leaves may or may not be spotted and are of two kinds: lower ones are broad, blunt, oval, forming a rosette; upper ones are longer, narrower, wavy, growing on flowering stem. Flower spike is tall, with a dense concentration of flowers. Individual flowers have a three-lobed lip with a pattern of spots; flower colour can vary from pale pink to light purple.

STATUS AND COMMENTS
Common, and found throughout Britain on calcareous soils.

SPOTTER'S CHART

LOCATION	DATE/TIME

GREATER BUTTERFLY-ORCHID
Platanthera chlorantha

FACT FILE

SIZE Height to 60cm **HABITAT** Shady scrub, woodland **FLOWERING PERIOD** May–Jul **HABIT** Upright perennial

IDENTIFICATION

Leaves are of two kinds: lower ones comprise a pair of broad, blunt ovals; upper ones are much smaller, growing on flowering stem. Flower spike is tall, with a scattering of flowers. Individual flowers are creamy greenish white with spreading petals, a long lip, and a long spur at back.

KEY FACT This beautiful orchid often has a lovely scent, but not every plant is scented. The very similar Lesser Butterfly-orchid grows in a wider variety of habitats, including on acid soils.

STATUS AND COMMENTS

Found throughout Britain, but common only in some places; usually on calcareous soils.

SPOTTER'S CHART

LOCATION	DATE/TIME

COMMON TWAYBLADE
Neottia ovata

FACT FILE

SIZE **Height to 40cm** HABITAT **Scrub, woodland, banks, grassland** FLOWERING PERIOD **May–Jul** HABIT **Upright perennial**

KEY FACT
Twayblades often go unnoticed, even when growing in large colonies. This is partly because, along with many other British orchids, they merge inconspicuously into their surroundings.

IDENTIFICATION
Leaves comprise a pair of large, broad, blunt, deeply veined ovals; glossy green. Flower spike is tall, with flowers along its length, often in large numbers. Individual flowers are modest: small, greenish, and with a dangling forked lip.

STATUS AND COMMENTS
Found throughout Britain, and probably our most common orchid.

SPOTTER'S CHART

LOCATION	DATE/TIME

FACT FILE

SIZE **Height to 40cm** HABITAT **Shady woodland,**
most often **Beech** FLOWERING PERIOD **May–Jul**
HABIT **Upright perennial**

IDENTIFICATION

Leaves are brown, papery, scale-like. Flower spike is yellowish brown,
with yellowish-brown flowers in a thick cluster at top, and in ones and
twos lower down. The plant feeds on rotting material, using a symbiotic
relationship with a fungus to do so.

STATUS AND COMMENTS

Although Bird's-nest Orchid has
been found in most parts of Britain,
it is only ever locally common.
It probably often goes unnoticed
in the depths of dark woods.

KEY FACT

This strange-
looking plant gets all its
nutrients from the soil, and
therefore does not need green
leaves. It takes its name from its
roots, which are said to
resemble a Magpie's nest.

SPOTTER'S CHART

LOCATION	DATE/TIME

WHITE HELLEBORINE
Cephalanthera damasonium

SIZE Height to 50cm **HABITAT** Shady woodland and scrub, most often Beech **FLOWERING PERIOD** May–Jul **HABIT** Upright perennial

IDENTIFICATION
Leaves are narrow, oval to lanceolate, and upwardly angled; all are on stem, becoming smaller towards top. Flowers are creamy white; they appear from leaf axils towards top of stem and look rather like fattened, half-open buds.

STATUS AND COMMENTS
Most common on calcareous soils in S England, White Helleborine is absent from much of the rest of Britain. It is a plant of woodland and scrub.

KEY FACT
Where it does grow, White Helleborine can appear in quite big colonies. It is a plant that might surprise by gracing an unpromising, neglected and forgotten scrubby area.

SPOTTER'S CHART

LOCATION	DATE/TIME

SWORD-LEAVED HELLEBORINE
Cephalanthera longifolia

FACT FILE SIZE **Height to 50cm** HABITAT **Woodland and scrub; occasionally in more open areas** FLOWERING PERIOD **May–Jun** HABIT **Upright perennial**

IDENTIFICATION

Leaves are long, narrow, slightly wrinkled and folded, often bent at tips; all are on stem, becoming smaller towards top. Flowers are white, often appearing in large numbers up stem, and with a half-open appearance (but more open than White Helleborine).

KEY FACT Sword-leaved Helleborine is also known as Narrow-leaved Helleborine. Similar, and also uncommon, is Red Helleborine, which has pinkish-red flowers and shorter leaves that do not bend at the tips.

STATUS AND COMMENTS

Most often found on calcareous soils in S England, Sword-leaved Helleborine is absent from most of the rest of Britain, and is not common anywhere.

SPOTTER'S CHART

LOCATION	DATE/TIME

BROAD-LEAVED HELLEBORINE
Epipactis helleborine

FACT FILE

SIZE **Height to 80cm** HABITAT **Woodland and scrub** FLOWERING PERIOD **Jul–Sep**
HABIT **Upright perennial**

KEY FACT
With its spike of subtly coloured flowers, Broad-leaved Helleborine is a striking sight. The flower colour varies from area to area. Closely related but rare is Dark-red Helleborine, a shorter plant with glorious wine-red flowers.

IDENTIFICATION
Leaves are oval, slightly folded and wrinkled; all are on stem, with the largest at the mid-point. Flowers appear purplish greenish pink from a distance (a closer look reveals that each flower component is a different colour); they are often produced in very large numbers at top of stem.

STATUS AND COMMENTS
Locally common throughout much of Britain.

SPOTTER'S CHART

LOCATION	DATE/TIME

FACT FILE

SIZE **Height to 80cm** HABITAT **Woodland and scrub** FLOWERING PERIOD **Jul–Sep** HABIT **Upright perennial**

IDENTIFICATION
Leaves are lanceolate, veined, upwardly angled; all are on stem, with the largest leaves at mid-point; grey-green with a violet tinge, as is the stem. Flowers are a combination of pinks, purples, whites and greens. The plant is often many-stemmed.

> **KEY FACT**
> Finding any orchid is exciting, but discovering a Violet Helleborine in full flower in late summer is really something special, especially when there are several flowering stems together.

STATUS AND COMMENTS
Found in S England and on calcareous soils.

SPOTTER'S CHART

LOCATION	DATE/TIME

Common names are in plain text and scientific names are in *italic*.

PHOTOGRAPHIC ACKNOWLEDGEMENTS

Photographs supplied by Nature Photographers Ltd. All photographs by Paul Sterry except for the those on the following pages:

TD Bonsall: 51; Brinsley Burbidge: 20, 144; Andrew Cleave: 15, 118.